MW01241267

INNER
POWER

*Women's Pertinent Role in Politics, War, Peace
and Nation- Building*

Amb. Hanna Dijok

Edited by Daniel Okello

Copyright © 2023

Amb. Hanna Dijok

All rights reserved. No part of this publication may be reproduced in any form or by any electronic, photographic, or mechanical means, including information storage and retrieval systems, without permission in writing from the author, except for 'fair use' as brief passages embodied in articles and reviews.
First published in May 2023 by Afrogate LLC
ISBN:
978-1-959037-12-5 (Paperback)
978-1-959037-20-0 (eBook)
For information about special discounts for bulk purchases, please contact the author:

Amb. Hanna Dijok

Acknowledgment

No achievement in life is possible without the help of many known and unknown individuals who have impacted our lives. We owe every measure of our success to the array of input from many people. Such is the case with this book about the role of women in politics, war, peace, and nation-building. It would not have been possible to write about such an intimate, broad, and profound subject without the selfless, dedicated, and kindhearted contributions of the following:

My friends Mr. Bol Jock, and Mr. Gatwech Ruot Nyoat for their contribution to this book project.

I am greatly indebted to my editor, Mr. Daniel Okello, whose meticulous eye combed through my manuscript to make it legible. May God's favor be with you.

I would also like to express my gratitude to my beloved and ever-supportive husband, Ezekiel Kan Kumban, whose cooperation and encouragement help me complete this project on time. You have been such a lovely companion on life's way.

My special thanks go to Prof. PLO Lumumba, the president and founder of the PLO Lumumba Foundation for contributing the foreword to this book.

Thank you, and may the heavens shower you with blessings endlessly! I would also like to thank the Afrogate publishing

team for the book cover's design, website, and publishing process. I'm very grateful.

Dedication

I dedicate this book to the strongest woman and gentle soul I know, my mother Mary Nyawanglal Lul Kuoth who taught me to trust in God and believe in hard work. Mother, you have made a huge impact in my life. I would not be the person I am today without you. You inspire me to be the best version of myself. Thank you for your guidance, your love, and your prayers.

About The Author

Amb. Hanna Dijok, a wife and a proud mother of three wonderful boys, Thon 15, Kabiel 12, and Andrew Kongo 7 years old. Amb. Dijok is an inspiring woman passionate about people's development. Born in South Sudan in the late seventies to Mrs. Mary Nyawanglel Lul kuoth and Dr. Andrew Kongo Dijok, Amb. Hanna Dijok would later move to Khartoum in Sudan with her mother and her siblings after the tragic death of their father. She later moved to Kosti City in the White Nile. Her mother became the only person that they could look up to—their strength and source of comfort. Her upbringing has shaped the woman she is today.

In 1997, Amb. Dijok left Sudan for France to join her elder sister, and a few years later, the rest of the family moved to Australia. Despite spending most of her life abroad, Amb. Hanna Dijok has maintained a strong connection to her country, South Sudan.

A seasoned women empowerment and peace advocate, today, Amb. Hanna Dijok is a successful entrepreneur, and a founder and CEO of the South Sudan Institute for Research and Advocacy, an organization that pursues pathways to reconciliation and sustainable peace and development in South Sudan.

Amb. Dijok has actively participated in peacebuilding by engaging vulnerable women and girls, through Sister's Hope for South Sudan, and Africa Peace Mediation and

Reconciliation Institute, having co-founded both organizations.

In 2016, she started a program for Internally Displaced People in the UN camps in White Nile (Sudan). The program was designed to empower widows and strengthen their skills in business, public health, and personal development to increase their self-esteem. Many women benefited from it.

Her Excellency Ambassador Dijok is also a United Nations Peace Ambassador through WOLMI organization, and a participant of the International Consulting Cabinet (I.C.C.); Women's Leadership & Affairs Department of WOLMI. She also conducted a series of intensive training in Protocol & Diplomacy and Humanitarian Diplomacy from the prestigious WOLMI Academy in Association with CICA International University & Seminary of Toronto, Canada. Additionally, Amb. Dijok holds a degree in Languages and French Culture and Civilization from Nantes University in France, and a certificate in Fashion Design from the School of Fashion Design in Paris.

After serving as a City Commissioner for the Nantes Mayor's Office on Council for Citizenship for Foreigners, and as an Advisory Board Member for Diaspora under French former Prime Minister Jean Marc Ayrault (France), Amb. Dijok was among the first people who worked at the South Sudan Embassy in Paris, France after South Sudan's independence.

As a peace advocate, Amb. Dijok's mission is to help people in need regardless of their nationalities or gender. She committed herself to being among those who work day and night to make

our world a better place. She strongly believes that the inclusion of women in peace and nation-building processes is essential for long-term success. That gender-equal participation contributes to longer, and lasting peace after conflict.

Foreword

Iread Thomas Hardy's Book, "The Mayor of Casterbridge" as a young man and I always remember this quotation:

> Her experience had been of a kind to teach her, rightly or wrongly, that the doubtful honor of a brief transit through a sorry world hardly called for effusiveness, even when the path was suddenly irradiated at some half-way point by day beams rich as hers. But her strong sense that neither she nor any human being deserved less than was given, did not blind her to the fact that there were others receiving less who had deserved much more. And in being forced to class herself among the fortunate she did not cease to wonder at the persistence of the unforeseen, when the one to whom such unbroken tranquility had been accorded in the adult stage was she whose youth had seemed to teach that happiness was but the occasional episode in a general drama of pain.

The meaning of this famous passage comes alive when I read *"Inner Power"*. In a succinct manner, Amb. Dijok grapples with the evergreen subject of conflict and peace building and the role of women. Without being prescriptive, Amb. Dijok isolates the unique qualities that she believes equip women with the wherewithal to be purveyors of conflict resolution and peace building.

Amb. Dijok's work also reminds me of those famous words of Professor Ali Mazrui in his documentary *"The African: A Triple*

Heritage", when he opined that the paradox of human society is that, <u>we revere women as our mothers, adore them as our wives and cherish them as our daughters"</u> but that in times of <u>war and conflict, we dehumanize them as if they were children of a lesser God.</u> The answer to this conundrum defies a simplistic answer but Amb. Dijok hazards an answer when she says at Chapter 7:

> *If we are to fight discrimination and injustice against women we must start from the home for if a woman cannot be safe in her own house then she cannot be expected to feel safe anywhere.*

The discernible thesis of Amb. Dijok's work is that for lasting peace to be achieved, women must be incorporated in the struggle. Indeed, she aptly identifies the United Nations Security Council Resolution 1325 which recognizes that women must be involved in peace building at every level as a *condition-sine-qua non* to lasting peace.

Amb. Dijok has written after the year 2020 which was designated by the African Union as the year of "silencing the guns" and at the beginning of a new decade in 2021 when the African Union has once again designated the period as the decade of "silencing the guns".

It is noteworthy that Amb. Dijok has given pride of place to women's participation in decision making. It cannot be gainsaid that women constitute an integral part in society and that their intimate involvement in matters of governance is a prerequisite to the total development of society. Indeed, it is gratifying that while the struggle for further participation of women in governance continues, it is now universally acknowledged that society can only ignore them at its peril.

Amb. Dijok's work is *ipso facto* emblematic because despite the best intentions of the best of her Sons and Daughters, Africa is still afflicted by conflicts in various parts including the Southern Cameroons (Ambazonia), Central African Republic, Eastern Congo, Nuba Mountains, Blue Nile and Darfur in Sudan, Somalia, Northern Mozambique, Libya and Tigray in Ethiopia. Most of the Sahelian region labors under conflicts of different intensity and it is women and girls that endure the most of the conflict as refugees or internally displaced persons. Perhaps it is this that justifies the title *"Inner Power"* because it is this power that gives birth to resilience.

On the basis of extant evidence, I agree with Amb. Dijok that there is great merit in involving women in the effort to resolve conflict and to build peace.

PROF. PLO- LUMUMBA, LL.D, D. Litt (hc), D.Sc (hc) FCPS (K), FKIM, FAAS (hon)

Preface

There are faces I recall and find severely disturbing, experiences I wish I could lock out of my head, ghosts of places I know and have lived. There is a knot tied around my heart, tightened around Polaroid pictures. These things are so shameful. They are secrets I have taken to bed for all these years. They are things that wake me every day and stir those memories to life. They have become the things I wish I could change.

I remember looking in her eyes and aching. A bitter, long-nurtured ache, a pain I nursed since then. Nyakouth was less than a week old when her mother died. The pupils of her clear-watered eyes were not wide enough to sink in the weight of grief spelled out for her infant self. Her skin, still tender and fragile to bear the scars of loss.

Nyakouth, daughter of God, however young and tender was just a number. Another motherless child from a hungry, sick, and homeless population on the run. Her eyes, however clear-watered, couldn't save her. They were merely statistical proof for the hopeless disillusioned people the war had made us. She would soon grow in the company of other children at our home. Children just like her. Some were orphaned by the war, others whose mothers had died in labor, and others who had come flocking to our home with their parents and grandparents, uncles, and clan heads seeking refuge, a place to stay and food to eat.

On the eve of the war, the only pain I had known was the loss of my father, Dr. Andrew Kongo. How his tragic death had been difficult for my widowed mother to deal with the many truths it had compelled us to face. How long it took my young self to accept its reality and how we had eventually moved into Khartoum to start over.

While living in Khartoum, mother resolved to go back to school and study midwifery; the science of enabling pregnant mothers to deliver their babies with ease. In 1989, she got a job with Medecins Sans Frontieres (M.S.F), or *Doctors Without Borders,* which required us to move to the White Nile city of Kosti.

Kosti lay on the western bank of the White Nile and was flung South of Khartoum. It had become a refugee hotspot given its huge refugee population. People fleeing the turmoil in Southern Sudan sought refuge there. They were hurled into crowds of wounded men, and women who had witnessed their husband's deaths and lost their children from war, and kala-azar disease. People whose survival entailed more grief than their misery.

Mother served there as a midwife. She spent her life there walking between rows of women whose bellies bulged with children conceived during the war—mothers to the generation of Southern Sudanese children who would grow to learn that their identity was the root cause of their suffering. She saved many infants and many mothers died from kala-azar. Nyakouth's mother was one of such cases. On the morning of her last day, she had held onto my mother's arm and

whimpered although with difficulty. "Mary Nyawanglel, please keep my child. My life is far spent. Promise me that you will take care of my child."

Nyakouth became one of the several orphans mother had taken into her care. During this time, mother hopped onto a second job and the third one too so that ends would meet. At the age of thirteen, I became a second mother to my four siblings and to the other children who were still in their infancy, while mama worked herself day and night. I had to change and take on evening classes after my siblings were back from school. My grandmother's help with the infants was extremely invaluable. She carried them, fed them, and soothed them to sleep.

Every day that passed, I saw and heard more about the war, and kala azar disease through the eyes of the women at our home. These women talked of their experiences after the war had come. They had prayed for the earth to split and swallow them alive. It didn't. They waited for the sound of gunshots to come whining about like an angry lot of wasps. They didn't. They thought the wall paint would peel off and shrink into hiding from the naked rage of war. It still did not happen. They were instead left holding onto their husbands' bodies, weeping and sneezing.

Their men were killed yet they were only raped and left to nurse that trauma the rest of their lives. They had seen their children's bodies burnt and blackened by enemy fires. The images of their peers are still rooted within their jagged memories. Their shadows followed them around in their sleep. Their voices

loomed within the hanging despair of their conversation; they seemed to respond through the echoes.

The women usually sat in circles with their children straddled to their chests and sang songs they had sung on their journeys here. They sang of land they had once belonged to, an identity they had been identified with, people they knew too well. Yet the things they sang of were things they had lost so. They yearned for a belonging—a place they would call home, set up huts, and rear their cattle again. They casually chorused: we don't belong here, but does it matter where we belong?

Later in life, I would have to learn about these experiences in books of history, in peace lectures about a new Sudan, from newspaper stories where the roles of these women, their efforts, and dreams of that Sudan were not even implied. Their names would be buried in the bleakness of the past and they would remain unknown to that generation they helped give birth to.

The war was fought by men, but women fought too. They cooked for the soldiers and nursed their wounds, they cared for the elderly and the children. They set up camps and traded spy intelligence from the enemy forces. They gave up all they had and compromised their dignity for a peaceful nation. Women's contribution went beyond any measurement during these civil wars, they have made significant sacrifices to the birth of their nation. Unfortunately, the world will only remember them as helpless victims of a war they had solely been part of.

It is important to note that despite these challenges, women have continued to take on the lead in the affairs of their nations; most notably Mama Rebecca Nyandeng de Mabior, the Fourth Vice President of South Sudan, known as "Mother of the Nation", whose efforts led to the establishment of an NGO named Widows, Orphans and Disabled Rehabilitation Association of New Sudan (WORDANS). WORDANS offered vocational training to all those affected by the struggle. It would later release a workforce of tailors, plumbers, electricians among other professionals. Ironically, even the nationalist wave of her husband couldn't eclipse her works.

I then learned of Prof. Julia Aker Duany, the current South Sudan Undersecretary of the Ministry of Public Service, whose sensational activism had founded the National Volunteers Program in 2010, one of the fundamental reasons for the 52% win in the pre-independence referendum. Her keynote address on lost boys and girls of Sudan: The Militarization of African Children, was pivotal to shaping discussions on the welfare of children in post-conflict states all over the continent.

The achievements of Hon. Rebecca Joshua Okwaci in governance as minister for Telecommunications and Postal Services and also an advocate for women through the Sudanese Women Voice for Peace are a mustard seed in concretizing the female hold of influence in peace-building. They are as well a cause for a women-owned future in the fields of peace and security, formerly dominated by the men.

Those images from my childhood have shaped my dream. I have wanted to give a chance to the grandchildren of those

women I saw. I have wanted to create a better world for them, for women to be regarded beyond the limits of femininity. Resolutions have indeed passed, initiatives have been started, policies and an action plan put in place to push for a women-led agenda in peace building, but these have still had loose ends and proved inadequate which demands a collective effort from both men and women across all generations. I am requesting all of you to help me realize a world where women are a core and indispensable part of peace and stability. This book is, therefore, a cradle of the infinite possibilities for women in war, peace, and nation-building.

Introduction

Women play a very vital role in human progress and have a significant place in society. Throughout history, the central role of women in society has ensured peace, stability, progress and long-term development of nations. However, these roles have always been hushed, ignored or uncelebrated, as women are treated as second-class citizens in many cultures across the world.

In this book, I call for original approaches to international policies that are designed to address the issues of the day and advance new ground in the global agenda for gender equality and the attainment of women's rights. I also demonstrate the developing acknowledgment of the untapped potential of women and their leadership. Indeed, throughout the course of recent years, the number of women in parliaments throughout the world has tremendously increased. Some countries have witnessed a surge of women elected to leadership positions, like Sub-Saharan Africa. However, I argue in this book that despite this progress, the overall global representation is still staggering below the 30 percent benchmark set as the irreducible minimum level of representation necessary to attain a "critical mass". This also implies that the number of women in leadership does not commensurate with women's population all over the world. Therefore, there is a need for an equitable involvement of women in all leadership positions in order to create and maintain vibrant and firm democracies.

The question we need to ask is where did the rain start to beat us? Long before and during the European colonization of Africa, ancient kingdoms and empires thrived for centuries on the continent. Some were headed by women, including female warriors who led armies against invading European powers to defend their people from conquest and enslavement. Even though women have been at the forefront of impressive exploits in combat, their stories are often overlooked and forgotten. In this book, I intend to remind ourselves about the women who have fought in the frontline and played active roles in liberating their people from oppression and armed conflicts especially in South Sudan side by side with men. There is a need to tell the forgotten history of South Sudanese women and from across the world who have played a critical role in the liberation struggle for independence of their countries in particular, and the world at large—the women of the world.

I also intend to show how women have brought positive change across the world using protests. Protest is a universal language. When many people with a common agenda come together to air their grievances, regardless of where they are, it is considered a powerful showcase of unity, strength, desire, and unity for change. Numerous women all over the world have played critical roles in planning and participating in protests globally. In the US, for instance, the struggle for women's suffrage started with the protests calling for women's rights in the mid-nineteenth century. However, women's tremendous roles in these protests and movements are usually overshadowed by men. In other words, men get credit and more limelight for their successes as opposed to women. In

this book, I highlight a few examples of the women's marches and protests across the world in the fight for fairness, human rights, and equality. I also illustrate how armed conflicts and ethnic cleansing bring their distinct forms of violence against women with them. I explore the issue of gender-based violence and rape as a weapon during the war using South Sudan Civil War as a case in point. I bring to light the reasons why rape is widely used in wars and its implications for peace in South Sudan. I also give instances of rape against women elsewhere in the world and illustrate its relationship with rape in South Sudan Civil War that has raged the country. The key questions that are intended to be answered in Chapter Seven of this book, therefore, include: What motivates the soldiers to rape women, girls, and boys? What makes the sexual violence in South Sudan different from similar atrocities committed in other countries during the war? What will the implications of rapes do for peaceful co-existence among the communities torn apart by war?

It is obvious that stopping a war or conflict is not the same as putting a permanent end to violence. An end to violence marks the beginning of the daunting task of building sustainable peace. This is a long-term process of encouraging people to talk, repairing relationships, and reforming institutions. Protecting civilians, promoting security, reducing violence, and assisting local authorities to take on these activities to promote long-term stability and development, are some of the peacekeepers' roles from the UN and other agencies. For positive change to last, everyone affected by a destructive conflict must be involved in the process of building peace. In this regard, women are critical to peacekeeping success around

the world. In the final Chapter of this book, I share firsthand experiences of women who overcame atrocities committed against them during war and how they built their lives, contributing to their nations' economies.

Table of Contents

Chapter 1:
THE PLACE OF WOMEN IN THE WORLD'S HISTORY

"Girls are capable of doing everything men are capable of doing. Sometimes, they have more imagination than men." — Katherine Johnson, mathematician and one of the first African-American women to work as a NASA scientist.

In the majority of the world's set of experiences, and across many societies, women have been treated with contempt. Their roles and contributions have been hushed while that of their male counterparts amplified. Yet there is nothing a man can manage without a woman. People were and remain first friends and mutual partners. They have always worked together to build and transform their world. When men went out to hunt for game meat, women gathered fruits and vegetables, and together they made a healthy meal for the family. Historical artifacts were built by both men and women. Why is the role of women either ignored or discussed in hushed tones? Why are women always kept in the shadows?

Many women did exceptional things, lived fascinating lives, and experienced interesting periods of history. What people have recorded as history, however, has often been the history of power. The battles. The kings. Politics and economics. History was white, elitist, and male. History was almost universally 'his story'. Since women were mostly barred from

power, what they did was rarely recorded. Until the 1970s most histories were written by and about men. Historians and archaeologists often assumed that most women's activities had been domestic, unvarying, and uninteresting and were therefore not worth recording or researching. Because of the way history was thought about, women's history was not seen as 'real' history.

History helps us to make sense of who we are and gives us a sense of identity. If children are taught a history of largely male achievement, they receive the message that women are not as important, or successful, or able to achieve as much as men. Girls and women need role models in history; otherwise, their expectations and sense of what is possible are limited. The neglect of women's histories perpetuates the inequality of the past.

In this chapter, I intend to highlight some of these uncelebrated contributions that women have made in different periods and talk about some of the women who made a difference during that period and left a mark in history, but who we might not hear about in history classes.

Women during the Foundation period

It is widely appreciated that many human civilizations occurred during this period in history, though there are little or no records. This is the Foundation era. It started with the first use of tools by Neanderthals, Denisovans, and early humans during the Stone Age. During this era, men and women served contrasting functions within their tribes. Men were generally

responsible for hunting, whereas women were generally responsible for gathering as well as caring for children and preserving tribal harmony. These roles were crucial for the general good of the community. In Paleolithic society, although there was a clear delineation of roles, men and women were largely equal in status as each appreciated one another's roles.

Then came the Bronze Age when humans settled in Mesopotamia, the Indus Valley, and ancient Egypt which saw the invention of the wheel and metalworking. The Bronze Age was a time of great cultural exchange between societies. This was the first time in history where ideas from one culture were regularly spread to other cultures. Studies of bodies from the Bronze Age show that women were responsible for this exchange! One study looked at 84 men and women who were buried between the end of the Neolithic Era and the beginnings of the Bronze Age. Two-thirds of these women traveled and lived in different places during their lives, but most of the men stayed close to home. Researchers assume that the women who traveled did so to spread technology, culture and start families. The most studied example of a Bronze Age woman is referred to as the Egtved Girl. Her body was discovered outside of Egtved, Denmark. She died around 1370 BCE and is estimated to have been between 16 and 18 years old when she died. Looking at the minerals in her hair and teeth, researchers have concluded that she traveled over five hundred miles between the place she was born and the place she died.

The Iron Age was a period that saw the formation of planned cities, the introduction of iron works, steel, and writing systems. In this society, women fought alongside men, as protection of their land and cities were seen as everyone's business. They were powerful, strong, and played important roles in response to the high stature, of which they were held. The status of women in these societies could be said to be much better than we might think. Women in ancient Egyptian society, for instance, enjoyed substantial rights. They could seek a divorce, own property and businesses, and practice and preach religion. It was only after the rise of civilizations and the rule of might that the status of women began to decline around the world.

Women during the Classical Era (600 B.C.-A.D. 476) and Middle Ages (A.D. 476 -A.D. 1450)

The Classical era, also known as Classical antiquity, began roughly around 600 B.C. in the majority of the world. It marked the beginning of a philosophical period in world history as well as the first recorded source of human history. Politically, the Classical era saw the rise and fall of most world empires. The Middle Ages is also known as the Medieval or Post-Classical era. Historians refer to the early part of this period as the Dark Ages due to the loss of recorded history after the fall of the Roman Empire in A.D. 476.

The ancient world included powerful women rulers, among them empresses, pharaohs, and queens. In 60 A.D, British Women called Boudica led a rebellion against the entire Empire of Rome according to Roman scholars (Tacitus and

Cassius). Boudica in British history was immensely powerful both in politics and the liberation struggle. Boudica took the throne when her husband passed on without a son to inherit his kingdom. While serving as the ruler, she resisted the Romans' humiliation under Roman Governor Suetonius Paulinus. Boudica stood up against the most powerful empire at the time and her actions led to her death. She sacrificed everything valuable for her to liberate her nation from foreign forces. Her two daughters were raped by the imperial army of Rome as a result of her rebellion against the system. She inflicted severe damage on the entire imperial Rome.

Another remarkable woman who lived during this time was Queen Tomyris of Massagatae. She stood firm against foreign invaders. She defended her people from King Cyrus II of Medes people and killed him on the battlefield in 530 BC (according to Greek historian Herodotus). Cyrus had despised Queen Tomyris at the very beginning simply because she was a woman but he got his fate at Araxes River. Like Boudica, Queen Tomyris took the throne of the Kingdom after the death of her husband. Cyrus sent Ambassadors with orders to court her pretending to make her his wife to annex Tomyris's Kingdom. However, Tomyris was aware that he was interested in her Kingdom and not herself. When Cyrus realized that he was rejected, he marched his army toward the River Araxes to build a bridge. However, Tomyris stood firm against this act to protect her Kingdom. She sent emissaries to advise Cyrus to back off. She was indeed a strong woman who stood against the most powerful state at the time. Cyrus was a ruler who had defeated men of great calibers. He earned a name for himself by use of power as he was feared by men. Like Boudica, her

son died in the conflict with Cyrus. When Cyrus refused to hide Tomyris' advice to keep off her Kingdom, the Queen assembled all the forces of her Kingdom and led them to the battlefield. Cyrus died on the battlefield after twenty-nine years of reign. Tomyris said to Cyrus's cold body that "I live and I have conquered you in the fight, and yet am I ruined, for you took my son with guile".

All 'grand temples and tombs and colossal statues bear many reminders of Egypt's ancient Queens and Female Pharaohs' (Barbara S. Lesko 1991, p 5). Cleopatra was both the last Pharaoh of Egypt and the last of the Ptolemy dynasty of Egyptian rulers. As she tried to maintain power for her dynasty, she made famous connections with Roman rulers Julius Caesar and Marc Antony. Another woman ruler who left a mark in ancient Egyptian history was Hatshepsut. She was born about 3500 years ago, and when her husband died and his son was young, she assumed the full kingship of Egypt. She even dressed in male clothing to reinforce her claim to be Pharaoh. She ruled Egypt from 1479-1458 BCE; longer than any king who ever ruled Egypt. The third ruler of the first Egyptian dynasty united upper and lower Egypt. Known only by name, there are also objects linked to this individual, including a tomb and a carved funeral monument. Many scholars believe that this ruler was a woman. Chief wife of Pharaoh Amenhotep IV who took the name Akhenaten, Nefertiti is portrayed in Egyptian art and may have ruled after her husband's death. The famous bust of Nefertiti is sometimes considered a classic representation of female beauty. Tacitus's History on Roman's campaign under Tiberius to conquer Germania in 9 A.D, has explained how much loyalty Barbarian Women were to their

cause. The Barbarian Women were far stronger, determined, and persisted to fight.

In Southern Sudan, Nyaguaec was a guardian Prophetess who guided Nuer leader Latjor Dingyan during the Nuer conquest to the eastern Nile in 1817 (Kelly 1986). When Nuer organized their expedition to the eastern Nile, Latjor Dingyan, Buoh Kapel, and Bidit Rialcar became their leaders. They led the rebellion against Chol Gey Diing. Latjor Dingyan was not able to make his expedition without the guidance of Nyaguaec. Nyaguaec was known as a woman with omniscient power to foresee the future. She made Latjor have confidence in himself by helping him foresee the unknown future.

Latjor made a plan to test Nyaguaec's ability to predict the future. He placed a small axe into his long hair to test if Nyaguaec would be able to know where the axe was. Latjor pretended to have misplaced his axe and pretended to look for it. While he was searching for it Nyaguaec asked Latjor, "Why do you pretend as if you did not know where you put your axe? You hid your axe in your hair, didn't you?"

 Latjor appreciated the unique talent in Nyaguaec. He knew that she would help him conquer the nations to the east. However, their expedition for conquest started in 1817 under the leadership of Latjor and Nyaguaec.

These women are classical examples of women who took up roles that were dominated by males and excelled. They complemented the men and gave them support. It is therefore laughable when one says that women cannot do what men can do.

Inner Power

History has proven beyond any reasonable doubt that there were many notable women throughout different eras who were able to break from societal norms to live the kind of life they choose for themselves and claim a position of power traditionally associated with males. They worked, ruled, and fought side by side with men. So, in the ancient world, no question doubted women's place in our humanity. Young women need to know such history to build confidence in themselves. But the structural process of human development has shifted to new institutions that seem to favor men over women. This shift has been done through practice which we can also change.

Queen Boudica in John Opie's painting Boadicea Haranguing the Britons

Queen Tomyris of Massagatae
Source: Alarmy

Queen Cleopatra was queen of the Ptolemaic Kingdom of Egypt
from 51 to 30 BC.
Source: Pinterest

Chapter 2:
WOMEN-CENTERED INTERNATIONAL POLICY

"Women belong in all places where decisions are being made. ... It shouldn't be that women are the exception."— *Ruth Bader Ginsburg*

International Policy unites various states linked directly following globalization. There exists a symbiotic relationship between one state and the other. In other words, no state can claim to be dependent upon itself in this century. This interdependence among the states, therefore, has a significant implication for international policy. This implies that decisions made by one state in the 21st Century have direct and indirect impacts on other states. And since a state doesn't exist in a vacuum, it means that the victims and beneficiaries of such decisions are the populations in these states which consists mainly of women and children. Yet contemporary International Relations theory and concepts continue to be dominated by males. In other words, men continue to make up the majority of key players in global politics as heads of governments, diplomats, and behind the scene actors. This begs the question: What role do women play in the global

decision-making table and what impacts do these decisions have on them? It is crucial to note that international policies are keenly crafted by the heads of governments to attain complex domestic and international agendas. Do women's interests dominate these agendas? Are women's voices heard? In this chapter, I will discuss the need for the paradigm shift to international policy from the current military security and global dominance to a women-centered approach.

Why women-centered international policy? And what is it about?

There is a growing call inside and outside of government for innovative approaches to policy that are tailored to address the issues of the day and advance new ground in the global quest for gender equality and the fulfillment of women's human rights. Despite measurable progress in some areas, such as girls' education, maternal health, and, increasingly, the repeal of discriminatory laws, there are new and dynamic challenges that threaten to reverse progress and roll back rights. And no country has achieved gender equality. The world faces an urgent climate crisis; persistent social, economic, and political inequalities and consequential trust deficits concerning globalization and the international institutions are seen to support it; reversals of legislative protections of sexual and reproductive rights; attacks on women; anemic progress on political inclusion of marginalized groups; and protracted political crises resulting in the largest forced displacement since World War II, among others. If we want to meet our human rights obligations, we cannot leave anyone behind, much fewer women and girls, in all their diversity.

It should be noted that the last three decades have seen dramatic reductions in global poverty, but not everyone has benefited equally. Hundreds of millions of people, especially women and girls, are still poor, have unequal access to resources and opportunities, and face major risks of violent conflict, climate and environmental hazards, and/or economic and political insecurity. There is a need for a protracted international agenda that aims to dismantle the male-dominated systems of international aid, trade, defense, immigration, and diplomacy that sideline women and other minority groups worldwide.

A women-centered international policy re-envisions a country's national interests, moving them away from military security and global dominance to position equality as the basis of a healthy, peaceful world. This is in keeping with Hillary Clinton's groundbreaking 1995 statement at the United Nations, "Women's rights are human rights."

By eliminating barriers to equality and helping to create better opportunities, women and girls can be powerful agents of change and improve their own lives and those of their families, communities, and countries. This is a powerful way to reduce poverty for everyone. The world could change in some positive ways if more countries, especially a power like the United States, made a concerted effort to improve women's rights abroad. Research shows that countries with more gender equality are less likely than other countries to experience civil war. Gender equality is also linked with good governance: Countries that exploit women are far more unstable.

In other words, supporting gender equality and the empowerment of women and girls is the best way to build a more peaceful, more inclusive, and more prosperous world. To do this, a good international policy should support targeted investments, partnerships, innovation, and advocacy efforts with the greatest potential to close gender gaps and improve everyone's chance for success. But it should also work across other action areas that reflect the multi-dimensional nature of poverty, in support of the Sustainable Development Goals. Working in this way leads to better development results and benefits everyone, including men and boys.

The policy should help protect and promote the human rights of all vulnerable and marginalized groups and increase their participation in equal decision-making. This will help women and girls achieve more equitable access to and control over the resources they need to secure ongoing economic and social equality. Committing to a women-centered approach to international assistance represents a significant shift in how we work. A women-centered approach is much more than focusing on women and girls; rather, it is the most effective way to address the root causes of global challenges such as poverty, climate change, civil wars among others. In other words, empowering women, overseas and at home, makes families and countries more prosperous.

Light at the end of the tunnel: Steps taken so far

A women-centered approach to international policy is already gaining ground across the globe. Significant steps have already

been made by the key players in global politics and policies; the powers that be.

The U.S., for instance, has taken steps toward a more women-centered international policy. The Biden administration has a woman, Vice President Kamala Harris, in its second-highest position. And that is not all. The Biden administration has declared its intention to "protect and empower women around the world." In the summer of 2020, under the Trump administration, the departments of Defense, State, and Homeland Security, along with the U.S. Agency for International Development, each published a plan putting women's empowerment in their agendas. These documents – passed per a two thousand United Nations Security Council resolution on women, peace, and security – promote women's participation in decision-making in conflict zones, advance women's rights and ensure their access to humanitarian assistance. They also include provisions encouraging American partners abroad to similarly encourage women's participation in peace and security processes. These are the components of a women-centered international policy. But the plans are still operating in boardrooms. A truly women-centered international policy would be coherent across aid, trade, defense, diplomacy, and immigration – and consistently prioritize equality for women.

In 2017, Canada launched a women-centered international assistance policy aimed at supporting women, children, and adolescent health worldwide. In January 2020, Mexico became the first country in Latin America to adopt a women-centered international policy. Its strategy seeks to advance gender

equality internationally; combat gender violence worldwide, and confront inequalities in all social and environmental justice program areas. Neither Canada nor Mexico has achieved its lofty new goals. Critics say Canada's lack of focus on men and boys leaves the traditions and customs supporting gender inequality not fully addressed. And in Mexico, which has among the world's highest rates of gender violence, it is hard to see how a government that cannot protect women at home can credibly promote women's interests abroad. But both countries are at least taking women's needs explicitly into account.

Africa has not been left behind. By devoting an entire Decade to women, African leaders have demonstrated their political will and commitment to promoting gender equality, women's empowerment, and women's rights. Throughout the Decade, considerable progress was made in translating commitment into measurable action as most African countries took giant steps to elevate the status of women through legal and constitutional means, institutional gender mechanisms as well as creating conducive environments for women to realize their potential.

As the evidence grows that women's well-being is central to everyone's well-being, the connection between gender equality and global security can be naturally incorporated into updated global strategies focusing on international security and human rights. These are the components of a women-centered international policy.

What should a truly women-friendly international policy be like? A call for action

I strongly advocate for Women- a centered international policy that underscores the importance of human dignity at a time when conflicts are multiplying and humanitarian principles, international laws, and human rights are increasingly under threat. An international policy that supports access to quality health care, nutrition and education, and principled, timely, needs-based humanitarian assistance that better addresses the particular needs and potential of women and girls.

I champion a women-centered international policy that maximizes the impact of our actions and helps eradicate poverty. An international policy that passionately defends the rights of women and girls so they can participate fully in society. An international policy that recognizes the fact that for our actions to be sustainable, we must ensure that they contribute to building local capacity. And that by eradicating poverty, we build a more peaceful, more inclusive, and more prosperous world. I firmly believe that promoting gender equality and empowering women and girls is the most effective approach to achieving this goal. A targeted approach to gender equality allows us to focus on initiatives that fight poverty and inequality by supporting gender equality and defending the rights of women and girls, particularly their sexual health and reproductive rights. Going forward, these initiatives should receive special, focused attention. A cross-cutting approach to gender equality means that all the international assistance initiatives, across all action areas, should be developed and implemented in ways that improve gender equality and

empower women and girls. This approach also means that all the implementing partners must consult with women and involve them in needs assessments, decision making, and planning of initiatives, as well as in the implementation, monitoring, and evaluation of projects.

Women and girls can achieve real change in terms of sustainable development and peace, even though they are often the most vulnerable to poverty, violence, and climate change. So, the countries across the globe should work closely with local women's rights groups, particularly in the areas of sexual and reproductive health; in the fight against the child, early and forced marriage; and in enabling access to the formal economy and decision making.

A women-centered international program promotes development and works for everyone. It targets areas such as sustainable agriculture, green technologies, and renewable energy. This will help increase women's access to economic opportunities and resources. Women and girls will achieve the economic independence they need to take control of their lives. It should be noted that women and girls are often the primary producers of food and providers of water, heating, and cooking fuel for their households. When these resources become more unpredictable and scarce due to, for example, extreme weather, women, and girls have to spend more time and effort attending to basic needs, such as growing food and collecting water and fuel.

The women-centered policy should also factor in the environment and climate action focusing on adaptation and

mitigation, as well as on water management. To promote Environment and Climate Action, international policy should support government planning and initiatives to mitigate and adapt to climate change, advance women's leadership and decision making and create economic opportunities for women in clean energy. Women often do not have sufficient funds to cover weather-related losses, nor do they have equal access to technologies that can help families and communities adapt to climate change. When women and girls have better access to climate-resilient resources and technologies, they can devote more time to the activities—such as education, paid work, political and public participation, and leisure activities— that enhance the quality of life for the entire community.

I advocate for women-centered international policy that promotes inclusive governance, including democracy, human rights, the rule of law, and good governance by providing a clear roadmap to end gender discrimination. An international policy that promotes and protects human rights, advancing the rule of law and building stronger institutions. An international policy that encourages greater political participation by women and girls.

A truly women-centered international policy helps strengthen global Peace and Security by supporting greater participation of women in peacebuilding and post-conflict reconstruction efforts helps to increase women's representation in the security sector, and enforces a zero-tolerance policy for sexual violence and abuse by peacekeepers.

The women-centered international policy does not leave men and boys out: it engages men and boys. Gender equality cannot be achieved by women and girls in isolation. Men and boys must also challenge the traditions and customs that support and maintain gender inequalities. Because social norms and gender stereotypes also limit men and boys in their societal and family roles, men and boys must be engaged in the fight for greater gender equality, be given opportunities to advocate for equality and be encouraged to lead by example in respecting and promoting the interests of women and girls. It is particularly important to transform the attitudes of adolescent boys, as gender constructs are shaped during adolescence. Engaging with adolescent boys provides the best opportunity to promote positive gender norms and prevent the perpetuation of negative stereotypes throughout their lives.

I look forward to developing countries that do not limit their international assistance strictly to a list of countries of focus, nor disperse their efforts in all directions but strike the right balance to ensure that their contributions have the greatest positive impact. International policies that address conflicts and climate change in fragile states and contexts, while continuing to foster economic development and growth that works for everyone in the poorest countries and supporting middle-income countries that face particular challenges, notably concerning governance. International policies that speak up for the poorest and most vulnerable, especially women and girls.

At this moment of increased nationalism, populism, and misogyny, it is time to call out backlash and call in new allies

and champions for gender equality and women's human rights, using all the tools at our disposal. As champions for gender justice from around the world honor the legacy of Beijing and launch the next generation of commitments to advance gender equality, and international policy that addresses women needs is one tool that shows promise for taking a much-needed, intersectional, and often multilateral approach to women's rights, simultaneously addressing urgent issues such as climate change, peace and security, inclusive growth, global health, and poverty alleviation. Every country can embrace a women-friendly international policy, no matter if it is a low, middle, or high-income one. At home and abroad, this approach could help to improve social development and reach social welfare and gender equality. Such an approach promotes inclusion, equality, peace, and security, both at the international and national levels.

Women who shaped International Policy

Several women across Africa and the world have played a significant role in shaping international policy. I will give a few examples.

Ellen Johnson Sirleaf

As Africa's first democratically-elected woman president, Ellen Johnson Sirleaf led Liberia through reconciliation and recovery following a decade-long civil war and responded to the Ebola Crisis of 2014-2015. She has won international acclaim for the economic, social, and political achievements of her administration, and, in 2011, she was awarded a Nobel Peace

Prize for her work to empower women. Under her leadership, the Ministry of Foreign Affairs successfully carried out its functions and responsibilities by formulating and implementing the Foreign Policy of the Government of Liberia and initiated actions to promote beneficial intercourse between Liberia and other nations including international institutions, as well as protected the rights and interest of the country abroad. The Minister of Foreign Affairs, Mrs. Olubanke King-Akerele, also oversaw the conduct of the Liberian Foreign Service. Today, Sirleaf is an influential voice for expanding women's political participation and involvement in decision-making processes. "Increasingly there is recognition that full gender equity will ensure a stronger economy, a more developed nation, a more peaceful nation. And that is why we must continue to work," she says.

Emtithal Mahomoud

Another woman who shaped international policy is Emtithal Mahmoud. She is a world champion slam poet and activist for the refugee cause. Born in Khartoum, Sudan, "Emi" – as she is known among her supporters– immigrated to the United States of America as a child with her family. She uses her talents to shine a light on the experiences of millions of refugees worldwide. "I use my words to raise the alarm on the conflicts of our time...in the hopes that someone might hear something that moves them," says Emi. In 2016, she was named a UNHCR Goodwill Ambassador and has visited refugee camps in Jordan, Uganda, and Greece, teaching poetry workshops and inspiring countless refugees to share their stories.

Meaza Ashenafi

Another significant African female figure in the global arena is Meaza Ashenafi, the first female Chief Justice of Ethiopia and a trailblazer in many ways, mainly for legal advocacy through her work with the Ethiopian Women's Lawyers Association (EWLA), an organization she co-founded with like-minded young female lawyers. After finishing law school at Addis Ababa University, of which she was the only female graduate from her class year, she served as a criminal court judge, which allowed her to see first-hand how the laws were discriminating against women. "When we founded EWLA 20 years ago, we did historic work of getting discriminatory laws, such as family law, citizenship law, pension law repealed. We brought the word 'Sexual Abuse' and 'Sexual Harassment' into the Amharic Language, as there were no words to describe them then," she says. Chief Justice Meaza is also a co-founder along with other female businesswomen of Enat Bank, the first bank in Ethiopia founded by female-majority shareholders, which she co-founded after noticing there was a lack of financial provision for women. "Leadership for me is having a vision and striving to achieve it. Women need to believe that they can do whatever they set themselves to do, despite society's pressure and people telling them otherwise. You can only have the power to be a change-maker if you believe in yourself," she says.

Susan Rice and Samantha Power

Susan Rice, former U.S. national security advisor, and Samantha Power, former U.S. ambassador to the United

Nations, are some of the women who shaped Obama's Foreign Policy. This is revealed in the two memoirs written by them. Rice became a U.S. assistant secretary of state at 32 and President Barack Obama's national security advisor at 48. Samantha Power succeeded Rice as Obama's ambassador to the United Nations.

Rice spent her entire life thinking about, and formulating, foreign policy; the mental habits of that world, both its aspiration and its limits, are second nature to her. She played a central role in all foreign-policy decisions in Obama's second term. As U.N. ambassador, she played an important role in deliberations over the reaction to Syrian President Bashar al-Assad's chemical attacks in August 2013. Though Rice had opposed arming the rebels or mounting a no-fly zone, she joined Power, Secretary of State John Kerry, and others in urging Obama to enforce his "red line" over chemical weapons with an airstrike.

Power also worked as a senior director of multilateral affairs and human rights at the National Security Council. According to Power, foreign policy is a tragic enterprise, a matter of choosing the lesser among evils. She has learned, she writes, that even if she cannot change the world, she can use the power she has been given to do whatever modest good she can. There is no mistaking the pathos of that acceptance. But what else is one to do? "Shrink the change" is the idealist's realism.

These are just a few examples of women who have risen against the odds to sit at the key global decisions making table that is still dominated by males. In the same vein, it is not

enough to have a few distinct female figures ascending to positions in international organizations such as the United Nations (UN), World Bank, or World Trade Organization (WTO), whilst men continue to make up the majority of key players in global politics. There is a need for increased participation of women as diplomats, scholars of international relations, and in leadership positions within institutions of global governance. The underrepresentation of women in international relations scholarship, diplomacy, and leadership undermines prospects for gender parity.

Amb. Hanna Dijok

Olubanke King Akerele, a Liberian politician and diplomat who served as the Minister of Foreign Affairs in the cabinet of Ellen Johnson Sirleaf from October 2007 until her resignation on 3 November 2010.
Source: Wikipedia

Meaza Ashenafi, the first female Chief Justice of Ethiopia.
Source: Borkena

Susan Elizabeth Rice, an American diplomat and policy advisor.
Source: Wikimedia Commons

Samantha Power, an Irish-American journalist and diplomat.

Chapter 3:
WOMEN IN POLITICS

"For me, a better democracy is a democracy where women do not only have the right to vote and to elect but to be elected,"—Michelle Bachelet

There is developing acknowledgment of the untapped potential and talents of women and women's leadership. Over the last two decades, the rate of women's representation in national parliaments globally has incrementally increased. Some regions have seen particularly dramatic increases, such as Sub-Saharan Africa, wherein in the last 20 years the number of women in parliaments has risen from 11 to 23.6 percent, and the Arab States region, which has seen an increase from 3.1 to 17.5 percent. Total global representation is still well below the 30 percent benchmark often identified as the necessary level of representation to achieve a "critical mass" – a considerable minority of all legislators with significant impact, rather than a token few individuals – not to mention falling short of women's representation as half of the world's population. The full and equitable participation of women in public life is essential to building and sustaining strong, vibrant democracies. Accordingly, the meaningful participation of women in national, local, and community leadership roles has become an

important focus on global development policy. Still, some may ask why it matters if women become political leaders, elected policymakers, or civil society activists. Why does the world need more women involved in all aspects of the political process? Women's political participation results in tangible gains for democracy, including greater responsiveness to citizen needs, increased cooperation across party and ethnic lines, and a more sustainable future.

Women's participation in politics helps advance gender equality and affects both the range of policy issues that get considered and the types of solutions that are proposed. Research indicates that whether a legislator is male or female has a distinct impact on their policy priorities. There is also strong evidence that as more women are elected to office, there is a corollary increase in policymaking that emphasizes quality of life and reflects the priorities of families, women, and ethnic and racial minorities. In the words of the National Democratic Institute's (NDI) Chairman Madeleine Albright, women in power "can be counted on to raise issues that others overlook, to support ideas that others oppose, and to seek an end to abuses that others accept." Further, it has been

found that more than men, women: work across party lines, are highly responsive to constituent concerns, help secure lasting peace, encourage citizen confidence in democracy through their participation, and prioritize health, education, and other key development indicators. Women's engagement is, therefore, crucial—and it is important to recognize that women are not a homogeneous group. Depending on whether women are young or older, educated or uneducated, live in

rural or urban areas, they have very different life experiences that lead to different priorities and needs. Moreover, not every woman elected to parliament or another legislative body will place women's issues or rights at the forefront of her agenda. Women's representation is not the only factor, but it is a critical factor for the development of inclusive, responsive, and transparent democracies.

So, why women in politics? The positive impact of women in politics is undeniable.

Kofi Annan noted, "study after study has taught us, there is no tool for development more effective than the empowerment of women. No other policy is as likely to raise economic productivity or to reduce child and maternal mortality. No other policy is as sure to improve nutrition and promote health, including the prevention of HIV/AIDS. No other policy is as powerful in increasing the chances of education for the next generation." Further, as Madeleine Albright has stated, the world is wasting a precious resource in the dramatic underrepresentation of women in leadership positions, often resulting in the exclusion of women's talents and skills in political life.

Male and female legislators must work together to solve the myriad of problems in their countries. To meet worldwide development goals and build strong, sustainable democracies, women must be encouraged, empowered, and supported in becoming strong political and community leaders.

Challenges facing women in politics

Throughout the electoral cycle, women can face numerous barriers to their effective participation and the fulfillment of their electoral rights. Their voices still go unheard, and their contributions are too often side-lined.

The United States, one of the most powerful and developed nations in the world, experienced a presidential race like no other in 2016 that pitied Hilary Clinton against Donald Trump. Hilary was the party's nominee for president in the 2016 presidential election, becoming the first woman to win a presidential nomination by a major U.S. political party. Clinton won the popular vote in the election, making her the first woman to do so. However, her campaign and career were shadowed by clear bias and discrimination due to her gender. It unearthed a scary showcase of the deep-rooted misogyny and patriarchal attitudes that are embedded in American society, and Clinton took the brunt of it — but she is not the only woman.

Throughout the world, women who dare to run for or be elected to positions of power are faced with hatred, discrimination, belittling, shaming, verbal abuse, mansplaining, and sexism. Traditional gender roles, gender-based stereotypes, and discriminatory attitudes and norms also act as major obstacles.

More challenges include the male-dominated model of politics that tends to undermine the value of women's contributions and their participation; lack of party support and exclusion from decision-making party structures; gender blind legal

framework; lack of campaign funds and financial resources; lack of formal or political education and limited access to information; lack of political experience; the dual burden and a disproportionate share of domestic work; lack of media coverage and gender-based stereotypes and bias in the media. In countries where candidates are responsible for deploying their party monitors during Election Day, there is a lack of party monitors safeguarding the interests of women's candidatures. Women also stay away from politics because of the perception that politics is a "dirty" game. Violence from within and outside the party also hinders women from taking part in politics.

As voters, women also face numerous challenges such as lack of ID and documentation required for voter registration, registration centers that are not accessible, near, or open inadequate time, and lack of information and awareness about voter registration procedures. Moreover, most women do not have access to information and awareness about voting, electoral processes, and overall political rights. Women also face family voting and pressure from family and community on the exercise of their political rights.

Women who participate in politics as civil society representatives (electoral observers, mediators, human rights defenders, social activists, etc.) are not spared either. They face traditional gender roles, gender-based stereotypes, and discriminatory attitudes and norms. Women are also underrepresented among electoral observers, mediators, etc. this excludes them from decision-making structures within civil society organizations. Violence from within and outside the organization also deter women from active participation.

Several models have been proposed to better understand how these barriers affect women in their political careers and professional development. Women politicians, as well as those working in EMBs and other organizations, frequently encounter the "glass ceiling", an organizational barrier understood as the "obstacles faced by women who aspire to hold high positions under equal pay and working conditions [...]." Another organizational barrier is the "glass wall", consisting of the horizontal segregation that relegates women to minor roles or denies them access to certain fields. The "cement ceiling", a barrier of psychological nature, refers to women's refusal to accept leadership positions because they think it would be difficult to balance personal and work life. Finally, the "sticky floor" is a cultural barrier that pushes women to deal with domestic chores and caregiving roles, which hinders their professional development.

African women who overcame political barriers

Some women have gone against the odds and triumphed in politics. In this light, modern-day icons like Angela Merkel, Kamala Harris, and Hillary Clinton are quick to come to mind. Fortunately, there are a lot more female leaders out there than common knowledge may suggest who pursued and achieved different political goals for their countries. Below are a few examples from Africa.

Ellen Johnson Sirleaf – Liberia

On 16th January 2006, thousands of Liberians poured along Monrovia streets to get a glimpse of Africa's first female elected president on her way to the inauguration. Dances and chants of 'we want peace … no more war' filled the air. At the front line were children and women waving and singing their hearts out. It was a new dawn for Liberians after about 14 years of civil war. To them, Sirleaf, the mother of Liberia, was the Messiah they had been waiting for.

She emerged victorious in the 2005 election and took an oath of office on 16th January 2006. This made her the first African woman to serve as an elected president of her country. She was re-elected in 2011 for the second and final term in the office.

Sirleaf became the president at a time when Liberia was in dire need of stability after decades of civil war and the Ebola crisis. She also inherited a country whose 80% of the population lived below the poverty level. After her historic inauguration on 16th January 2006, she immediately put Liberia on the reconciliation and economic recovery path.

Honorable Elizabeth Nyawal Chuol- South Sudan

Honorable Elizabeth Nyawal Chuol was a pharmacist before she became a politician. In 1976, she worked with my late father Dr. Andrew Kongo Dijok when he was a shift executive of both Malaka and Nasir's hospitals. Dr. Andrew Kongo was the first South Sudanese pharmacist during that time, and first pharmacist in the whole Upper Nile state.

"Dr. Kongo had a good relationship with people and was very passionate about his work. I remember working with him and how he would always go above and beyond for his patients. We worked together for a long time, and he was the one we would go to for all our medications needs. He truly had a good heart, and was loved by all who knew him". She says.

Honorable Elithabeth Nyawal Chuol was also among women who made remarkable contributions to Sudan's politics. She joined the political scene as early as 1982. Joining politics as a woman was meant to resist the establishment that undermined women's role in politics. The society of Sudan by then was under Islamic influence. A woman was not considered as a leader that could take part in Country's leadership but as a housekeeper. Women were seen as a Mother and a wife rather than a role model. That meant the first women to take up public duties like Honorable Nyawal had to face several barriers.

It took some women to work patiently to achieve women's freedom and secure political space for women. Hon. Nyawal has led the political struggle for women since 1982. She inspired women when she became a State Advisor in 1984 and later rose to the post of Deputy Speaker in the State Parliament. Her boldness to challenge the status quo has inspired more women, especially the younger generation, to join politics and make tremendous contributions in public service. She has proven that a woman can serve the public at any level and still remain a loyal wife to her husband and a caring mother to her children.

There is overwhelming evidence that women's participation in politics is beneficial to both their own communities and societies, and broader peace and stability. But despite the existence of a number of international conventions and legal frameworks guaranteeing women's political rights, we remain far from the goal of gender parity. Men are still dominant in the political decision making process. For example, in the structure of the SPLM political party, men are the majority in a higher organ called the Political Bureau.

Honorable Fawzia Yusuf H Adam- Somalia

Politics is a grueling path for women in Somalia. Despite the 30% seat quota for female lawmakers, Somalia politics is still a male-dominated affair, both at the local and national levels. Regional clan presidents have always disregarded the quota by blocking potential female candidates, leaving the quota unfilled. These, coupled with pervasive cultural and social barriers and clan-dominated systems, make it difficult for women to succeed in politics. Women are typically marginalized from the decision-making processes of their communities. For many, this means that their political dreams end before they even have a chance to begin.

However, there are a few brave and ambitious Somali women who have broken these cultural and social barriers to succeed not only in politics and governance but also academia. The most inspiring and significant of them all is Honorable Fawzia Yusuf H. Adam who swam against the tides to become Somalia's first female Foreign Affairs Minister and Deputy Prime Minister of the Federal Government of Somalia. She

acted as Prime Minister on three occasions. With over three decades of experience in the fields of Politics, International Relations, Public Policy, Diplomacy, United Nations, Management, Development, Education, Human Rights, Poverty Reduction, Humanitarian Relief Efforts, Women Empowerment, Business & Media, Honorable Fawzia Yusuf H. Adam has dared to vie for presidency in 2021-2024 presidential elections as the only female candidate.

Her candidature was informed by her tremendous contributions to the development of her country and advocacy for the rights of women and other marginalized groups. She believes that Somalia has untapped potential as a result of unending conflicts.

"Somalia has the longest coast in Africa. It has the highest per capita of livestock in the world, with over sixty million livestock. We have rivers flowing into the sea with millions of hectares of agricultural land, natural gas, oil, gold, diamond, rare earth, and all kinds of minerals. It is unbelievable what we have but tribal ego has destroyed my country," she says.

The lasting peace and the much-desired transformation can only be realized by patriotic and selfless women like her. A daughter of a liberation hero and a composer of Somalia's National Anthem, Honorable Fawzia has Somalia's interest at heart.

"We need to bring economic development. We should create jobs and stop the killings. A time has come to protect our kids and give them quality education and health. As we speak now, my people are dying of drought which is not natural. It is man-

made. They are manipulating our skies because we cannot control our skies. We are losing marine resources including fish worth billions through illegal international fishing and piracy. We cannot control our borders. We are losing all these resources. For that reason, I want to run for the presidency. If I win, we will change this and bring a paradigm shift in the Horn of Africa. I am proud to vie for the presidency and stand firm and tell them to stop the mayhem and bring peace, prosperity, and development to my people. Even if I get killed, I will die happily for my country," she said. "I am a role model to many Somali women. Even if I don't win, I want them to try next time. I want to inspire them to join politics and secure top government jobs in order to save our country. The country will not stabilize if women are marginalized. That is why I have decided to run and take a risk in such a risky political environment for women."

Honorable Fawzia Yusuf has proved through action that women, given a chance, can transform their country and lead it to prosperity. She has demonstrated this by successfully representing Somalia as a Chief Diplomat in major capitals in North America, Europe, Asia, Africa, the Middle East and the United Nations. Moreover, she has served her country as a member of parliament for more than 9 years. She also participated and played a major role in Regional and International conferences and meetings relevant to Somalia during her tenure as Foreign Affairs Minister. That period was filled with accomplishments that exhibited the rebirth of Somalia's diplomacy and restoration of Somalia's credibility.

Honorable Fawzia has not only broken the glass ceiling in politics. She has a robust background in academic world, with Masters in International Relations and Public Policy, SAIS- Johns Hopkins University, Washington DC, USA; Honorary PHD from University Popolare degli Studi di Milano, Italy; BA Education (Al Ahfad), Umdurman, Sudan; and Diploma in Print Media Studies- American University Paris. She is a founder of First Chancellor of University of Hargeisa Somaliland and Current Chair of National Democratic Party; Co- Founder of HIIGSI- a Coalition of 9 Political parties; Founder and CEO of RAAD TV International; Founder of RAAD Foundation NGO; Founder SOMAID an International NGO; Founder Association of Somali Women Advancement.(ASWA); and Co-Founder and first Chair of CSO (Umbrella group for Somali Diaspora community organizations in the UK). She is also a member of highly distinguished international Institutions. Her tremendous contributions have been recognized and celebrated both nationally and internationally through distinguished awards which include Somali Heroines Award given by Somali Women Leaders in Recognition of outstanding work during the Executive and Legislative positions held by Hon. F Adam; 202i; Award by Canadian Eye on Africa in recognition of Outstanding Achievement, work and endeavors for the people of Somalia, 2013; Award by the Somali Community, Minnesota, USA, in Recognition of the Establishment of University of Hargeisa just to mention a few.

Politics and academia have not made Honorable Fawzia to forget her duties as a respectful wife and loving mother. She has successfully raised three children; two boys, and a girl who

are well accomplished. Her late husband was a highly decorated General who also became a diplomat in France and the US.

Rebecca Nyandeng de Mabior – South Sudan

She became one of the Vice Presidents of South Sudan in the unity government in February 2020. After the death of Dr. John Garang, General Salva Kiir took over his positions and became the first Vice President of Sudan and the President of the Government of South Sudan and commander in chief of SPLM/A. General Kiir appointed Rebecca Nyandeng De Mabior as the Minister of Roads and Transport for the Government of South Sudan.

She continued to be a strong advocate for the implementation of the Comprehensive Peace Agreement signed by Dr. John Garang before his death on 30th July 2005. She continued to support the implementation of the peace process until the South attained independence on 9th July 2011. During that same year when her husband died, Madam Rebecca visited the United States of America and met with President George W. Bush. She offered a message of appreciation for the American involvement in the quest for peace in South Sudan. In 2009 President Obama continued the efforts with Secretary Clinton and Ambassador Rice to see that the peace agreement is implemented in Sudan.

Madam Rebecca also received an interview from NPR. She spoke of her commitment to the liberation of South Sudan while she also respects the necessity of a united Sudan under

the New Sudan Vision created by Dr. John Garang in 1983. She visited Grinnell College and Iowa State University, the Iowa universities where her late husband completed his education before the Second Sudanese Civil War broke out in 1983. Dr. John Garang and his wife Rebecca have six children who are active supporters of peace and stability in the new Republic of South Sudan.

Abuk Payiti Ayik- South Sudan

Abuk Payiti Ayik is a South Sudanese politician who has worked as a member of the country's Transitional National Legislative Assembly, representing the Sudan People's Liberation Movement and leading the Gender, Social Welfare, Youth, and Sports Committee.

Before independence, Abuk Payiti represented Malakal. She was also involved with the body's gender committee. She helped advocate for women's needs throughout the peace process and during the writing of the Comprehensive Peace Agreement with the government of Sudan. Payiti is affiliated with the Sudan People's Liberation Movement and has been involved with its Women Commission. After independence, she became a representative of Malakal County in Upper Nile State in the National Legislative Assembly.

As an advocate for women's rights, Payiti has also been involved in the South Sudan Women General Association and Sudanese Women Empowerment for Peace, serving as director of the latter's gender desk for the southern sector. She is widely known as a quiet but conservative lawmaker.

Governor Sarah Cleto Hassan Rial of Western Bahr el Ghazal State- South Sudan

Hon. Sarah Cleto Rial is celebrated as newly appointed female Governor in South Sudan. This did not happen by coincidence. Her immense contributions in the corridors of peace-building, leadership and conflict resolutions have demonstrated that women can make enormous contributions in the liberation struggle. Indeed, she is a force to reckon with. She is full of energy, unstoppable and unforgettable.

Hon. Sarah Cleto Rial has worked as the Executive Director and the brain behind Global Partnership for Peace in South Sudan (GaPPSS)—a non-profit organization that promotes peace throughout South Sudan and among South Sudanese living in the Diaspora. As a peace and human rights activist, Hon. Sarah Cleto has, for more than two decades, been at the forefront of organizing communities, and leading successful programs. These programs have built sustainable peace, promoted equal access to services, challenged harmful gender norms, and promoted women and girls' rights to education. She has also been actively involved in women's empowerment and wellbeing. Since 2011 to date, Sarah has also diligently served as a part-time finance administrator for South Sudanese Enrichment for Families (SSEF), Lincoln, Massachusetts. SSEF is the only whole-family resource dedicated to South Sudanese who have resettled in Massachusetts. She juggles this role alongside an equally demanding job as a program coordinator for Rippel Foundation, Cambridge, MA, a position she has held since 2017. Sarah has vast experience in program development and management—supporting the

strategic direction of large-scale programs, setting budgets, managing risks, building partnerships, and maintaining organizational governance.

Prior to her current appointment as a Governor, Sarah was the senior executive assistant to the CEO, Management Sciences for Health, Medford, MA (2016 – 2017), and strategy program analyst, South Sudan Enrichment for Families, Boston, MA (2015-2017). She also served as a program director for My Sister's Keeper, Boston, MA (2005 – 2016), a position where she directed educational and advocacy programs, supported local community programs in South Sudan and led international activism for peace in Sudan and South Sudan. In this capacity, she also promoted research on topics of mutual interest to scholars and policy makers in the Middle East and Africa. In addition, she assisted in daily office management, supported scholars, and organized a series of public lectures and conferences.

Through her endless efforts, expertise and leadership roles in different capacities, Hon. Sarah Cleto Rial advocates for the meaningful participation and leadership of women and their efforts towards silencing the guns, enhancing good governance, democracy, respect for human rights, justice, the rule of law towards a peaceful and secure Africa as outlined in Agenda 2063.

Aja Fatoumata C.M. Jallow-Tambajang- Gambia

Aja Fatoumata C.M. Jallow-Tambajang is a Gambian politician and activist who served as Vice-President of the Gambia and

Minister of Women's Affairs from February 2017 to June 2018, under President Adama Barrow. Early in her career, she had been the chair of the Gambia National Women's Council and an advisor to Dawda Jawara, the first President of the Gambia as a nation independent from the colonial rule of the British Empire. After the military coup d'état in July 1994 that deposed the Jawara government, she held the post of Secretary of State for Health and Social Welfare from 1994 to 1995 in the cabinet of the Armed Forces Provisional Ruling Council. She was appointed as Vice-President by Barrow in January 2017 but was found ineligible due to constitutional age restrictions. She was instead made Minister of Women's Affairs overseeing the office of Vice-President, until the constitution was changed and she was formally sworn in as Vice-President in November 2017. Before her appointment, she had served as chair of Coalition 2016, the alliance of opposition political parties that had supported Barrow's candidacy in the 2016 presidential election.

Aja had been advocating for women's rights for most of her life. She even engaged in political activism in the Gambia to press for freedom from the 21-year dictatorial regime of Former President, Yahya Jammeh. On her recent trip to the United States after being sworn in as Vice President, she said, "There was no freedom of expression or freedom of association. Institutions were dormant because of his dictatorial handling of the state. There were lots of political persecutions". She consistently fought for poverty alleviation, social justice, and equity. Because of her excellent mediation skills, Fatoumata was appointed as the mediator to engage with various opposition parties to realize gender balance. As a result

of these efforts, in 2016, she was appointed a chair of the coalition that pushed for regime change. After 2 decades of dictatorship under Yahya Jammeh, the opposition coalition finally won the election in December 2016. Jallow has worked with various international organizations such as the UNDP and various Women NGOs. Before being appointed Vice President to Adama Barrow, Aja Fatoumata Jallow held various high profile positions including Advisor to Gambia's First President on Women and Children Affairs and Chair of Gambia National Women's Council.

She worked in volatile, war-torn regions, and she was once a victim of a rebel hostage situation; she luckily survived the ordeal. Her passion for women's empowerment earned constant threats to her life, as well as the lives of her family. Her movements were also often monitored by the military. During her engagements, she had to negotiate with warlords and work in areas under rebel control to assist women.

Joice Mujuru – Zimbabwe

Born in 1955, Joice Teurai Mujuru is a famous Zimbabwean politician. Mujuru's role in Zimbabwe's independence fight has added to her cachet. She joined that battle in the 1970s before she had even completed secondary school. Efforts to overthrow the Rhodesian government included guerrilla tactics. According to some reports, her nickname during that era was Teurai Ropa, which in Shona means Spill Blood. When former President Robert Mugabe became Zimbabwe's leader in 1980, Mujuru was a key figure in his administration. In 2004, Mugabe passed over Emmerson Mnangagwa, who was the

front-runner for the office of vice president and named Mujuru to that position. Some of the portfolios she held included: Minister for Youth, Sport and Recreation between 1980 – 1985, Minister of State in the Prime Minister's Office between 1985-1988, and Minister of Community Development, Co-operatives, and Women's affairs between 1988 to 1992. In addition, she served as the governor for Mashonaland Central between 1992 and 1996.

Her political career has been marked by a host of other problems. She was personally sanctioned by the U.S. government in 2003 for taking part in efforts to undermine democratic processes, controls a farm that Zimbabwe's top court ruled was illegally seized, and she has dabbled in the illegal sale of large amounts of gold from the Democratic Republic of Congo.

In 2014, her continued criticism and frosty relations with ex Zimbabwe's President, the late Robert Mugabe, caused her expulsion from the ruling party. Along with losing her position as the Vice President, she also relinquished her Deputy Party leader position. The ruling party accused her of plotting to overthrow Robert Mugabe's government. After her exit from the ruling party, she formed a new political party, the Zimbabwe People First Party. "Today we confirm our existence as a viable, home-grown political party. Zimbabwe People First Party here. We are not fighting one man, but a system: that system which is unjust".

She was among the few women in Zimbabwe who managed to penetrate the country's political landscape and make her voice

heard, especially at a time when the country was recovering from war.

Sophia Abdi Noor – Kenya

Sophia Abdi Noor went down in history as Kenya's first elected female Member of Parliament from North Eastern Kenya. Considered to be a marginalized region, Sophia won the Ijara Constituency seat in Isiolo County, Northern Kenya, in the August 2017 election after beating the male incumbent, her closest rival. Born to a family of Somali pastoralists, the member of the 10th Kenyan Parliament became popular because of advocating for the rights of marginalized women. Noor has spearheaded and participated in numerous gender equality campaigns and was among the very few women from her community to complete high school and enroll in a teaching course.

For many years, communities living in North Eastern Kenya had always downgraded women and held strong conservative views against them. For instance, women's leadership was seen as taboo, both from a religious and cultural perspective. Because of this perception, the conservative Somali community was against women contesting for elective seats. Those who defied the odds typically had no financial resources to compete, were viewed as disrespectful of the culture and were often belittled.

The promulgation of Kenya's constitution encouraged Sophia to continue fighting for women's rights, which are now fully enshrined in the constitution. "The new constitution allows us

to openly seek votes, and I believe that recent civic education has sunk into the community because I campaign from village to village".

Noor is among the founders of Womankind Kenya, a group formed to advocate for issues about women and girl child education. Throughout her life, the former teacher has fought hard against retrogressive cultural practices such as early marriage, wife inheritance, and female genital mutilation.

She previously tried to run for the Ijara parliamentary seat in 1997 and 2013 but lost it. After graduating with a diploma in community development, she worked with numerous international organizations such as Oxfam, Save the Children, CARE International, and World Vision among others.

Her primary reason for contesting a parliamentary seat was to use parliament as a means to introduce legislation that would help to deal with challenges faced by women, especially those from marginalized regions. 1n 1997, her nomination was canceled due to cultural and religious arguments that prohibited women from becoming leaders.

Noor's journey of hard work and resilience has caused many women to benefit from her numerous initiatives. She has also won various international awards that recognize her efforts towards women's empowerment.

Diane Shima Rwigara – Rwanda

Diane Rwigara was born in Kigali in 1981, and she is known to be a fierce critic of Rwanda's President, Paul Kagame, and his

government. Rwigara, who is Tutsi, was born into a family of three. She came into the limelight after Assinapol Rwigara, her father and Kigali business tycoon, died mysteriously in a car accident in Kigali. Her dad was a key financier of the ruling party, the Rwandan Patriotic Front. She and her family believe their father's death was politically motivated.

The US-educated politician openly accused the government of masterminding her father's death. She sought help from both international human rights organizations and foreign diplomatic missions in Kigali to help her get justice. Rwigara is an accountant by profession; however, she is also a vocal women's rights crusader who has openly criticized the government for bad governance, oppression, and various forms of injustice.

In May 2017, Diane announced she was going to be a presidential candidate for the August 2017 elections. She intended to run on an Independent ticket, but things took a turn for the worse: nude photos of her were leaked online only 72 hours after her announcement. However, Rwigara was not deterred, and she accused the government of leaking the photos to humiliate and intimidate her. She insisted she would still go for the top seat and focus her energy on eradicating poverty, advocating for free speech, and championing human rights.

Unfortunately, her dream to run for the presidency was thwarted when the National Electoral Commission refused to clear her, claiming she didn't fulfill all the requirements. Rwigara found this move malicious and accused the

government of frustrating efforts by critics to vie in elections. "The RPF are scared," Rwigara said, "If they are loved by the people, as they claim, why is it that when someone like me announces an intention to run, they resort to all these dirty tricks to try to discourage me and silence me? If they were really popular, then they would have let me compete".

Diane has landed in trouble with authorities on several occasions. Immediately after the August elections, she was arrested and charged with numerous offenses- fraud and treason included. Even though she has faced so many challenges, Rwigara believes she is the voice for the voiceless, and her courageous and stubborn personality keeps her going.

Alengot Oromait – Uganda

In 2012, Proscovia Alengot Oromait made history by becoming the youngest individual in Africa, and globally, to be elected as a Member of Parliament. At only nineteen, Alengot won the Usuk County with 54.2% of the vote. She came into the limelight after the untimely death of her father, Michael Oromait, whose sudden death triggered a by-election.

Keen on fulfilling her dad's dreams for her to become a politician, Proscovia submerged herself in politics. Oromait was born in 1993 in Katakwi District and was the second born in a family of ten children. Since childhood, she showed great leadership traits. While at St. Kalemba Senior Secondary School, Alengot was a great and accomplished debater who actively involved herself in writing articles and taking photographs for the school magazine.

Her teachers knew she had great talent and exemplary skills, and they weren't surprised when they heard she was planning to succeed her father in politics. Some of the issues Alengot is passionate about include education, health policy, gender issues, and the environment.

"Leadership for me is having a vision and striving to achieve it. Women need to believe that they can do whatever they set themselves to do, despite society's pressure and people telling them otherwise. You can only have the power to be a change-maker if you believe in yourself," she says.

Those who know the family closely said she actively campaigned for her father and even often gathered youths, encouraging them to vote for him. She ended up missing school in the process but managed to play a key role in ensuring her dad won the Usuk County seat.

In 2013, Oromait was honored by Forbes. She was among the Top 20 Young Powerful Women in Africa. She admits her father was a major influence in encouraging her to take interest in politics, as he praised her for being talkative and educated. Alengot won her seat under the ruling party's National Resistance Movement. At the time she became an MP, she had finished high school and was waiting to join the university. She later joined Christian University in Mukono, where she studied Mass Communication.

While on campus, she had to balance her time as both a student and a legislator. Her decision to vie for a parliamentary seat and get into politics at such a tender age was admirable. Many praised her for her courage and ability to defy all odds. Alengot

was brave and forged on despite critics who argued her that candidature was a big joke and that she should have been in school chasing her career instead.

When asked how she manages her time, she said, "Because I am a Christian, I do not booze (take alcohol). My free time is for the Bible and reading my novels...that is how my life is".

Politics is an expensive affair and for one to succeed, the aspirants must have financial resources. Male politicians are preferred compared to female ones based on the societal value assumption that political activities are masculine and male candidates are believed to stand a better chance of winning elections. Under-representation of women in political seats or decision-making at the political party level means that the policies formulated are not geared towards the political welfare of the women and developments in the role of women. Societal norms are therefore one of the biggest hindrances to women's participation in politics. Political parties should be pressured by women's groups, party members, and representatives to include gender equality policies into their political programs.

Liberia's former President Ellen Johnson Sirleaf addressing her supporters, after she was released from prison in 1986.
Source: Africa at LSE

Honorable Elizabeth Nyawal Chuol
She's a professional Pharmacist, a Politician, and legislator. Currently she is a
member of the newly Reconstituted Transitional National Legislative Assembly
in the Republic of South Sudan.

Honorable Fawzia Yusuf H. Adam- Somalia
Former Deputy Prime Minister of Somalia

Rebecca Nyandeng De Mabior, a South Sudanese politician. She has been one of the Vice Presidents of South Sudan in the unity government since February 2020.
Source: Sudan Tribunes

The former US Secretary of State Hillary Clinton presents the Eleanor Roosevelt award for Human Rights to Sarah Cleto Rial.
Credit: AFP via Getty Images.

Aja Fatoumata C.M. Jallow-Tambajang, a Gambian politician and activist who served as Vice-President of the Gambia and Minister of Women's Affairs from February 2017 to June 2018, under President Adama Barrow.

Joice Teurai Mujuru, a famous Zimbabwean politician.

Amb. Hanna Dijok

Sophia Abdi Noor, Kenya's first elected female Member of Parliament from
North Eastern Kenya.
Source: Hivisasa

Diane Rwigara is a fierce critic of Rwanda's President, Paul Kagame, and his government.
Source: Therwandan

In 2012, Proscovia Alengot Oromait made history by becoming the youngest individual in Africa, and globally, to be elected as a Member of Parliament.
Source: Alchetron.com

Chapter 4:

WOMEN WHO INFLUENCED AMERICAN DEMOCRACY

"Anyone who claims to be a leader must speak like a leader. That means speaking with integrity and truth." – Kamala Harris

The history of women in American politics is just as long as that of the nation as a whole. It is rich and varied. As the nation grew, women's roles in government and political movements evolved as well, though it wasn't always easy. Women have been actively excluded from the political landscape for centuries, often having to fight or even inherit their way into a government role. Even in the days before the Constitution guaranteed women the right to vote, many tried hard to make a difference as best as they could — and succeeded, not only by breaking glass ceilings and proving that women could handle the job but also by introducing important legislation, standing up for their fellow citizens' rights and much more.

Whether they held office at the local and federal level, whether they were appointed to the most high-profile jobs in politics or to a role many would never hear about, and even if they merely ran and lost, each made her mark. Some of them wielded their influence in the nation's earliest days and others have only recently been elected to office. And, of course, that history is still being written by many women who have yet to make it to the history books.

It would be impossible to sum up the complete role that women have played in the history of American politics, especially considering the many female activists and thinkers who, though excluded from public office by nature of their gender, made a difference in the evolution of the nation's governmental and political narrative.

In this chapter, I take a look back at a few examples of influential American women who have helped define the history of American civic life.

Madeleine Jana Korbel Albright

Madeleine Korbel Albright, sworn in as the 64th United States Secretary of State in 1997, after unanimous confirmation by the U.S. Senate, became the first female Secretary of State and the highest ranking woman in the United States government. As Secretary of State and as U.S. representative to the United Nations before that, she created policies and institutions to help guide the world into a new century of peace and prosperity.

Concentrating on a bipartisan approach to U.S. foreign policy, she attempted to create a consensus on the need for U.S. leadership and engagement in the world. Among her achievements were ratification of the Chemical Weapons Convention and progress toward stability in Eastern and Central Europe.

Albright dedicated her life to international study. After receiving her B.A. At Wellesley College, she studied international relations at Johns Hopkins University before earning her M.A. and Ph.D. at Columbia University. Before her appointment as Secretary of State, she had a diverse career. Albright was Sen. Edward Muskie's Chief Legislative Assistant; a Woodrow Wilson fellow; president of the Center for National Policy, a nonprofit research organization; and Research Professor of International Affairs and Director of the Women in Foreign Service Program at Georgetown University's School of Foreign Service. During President Clinton's first term, Albright served as the United States' Permanent Representative to the United Nations and a member of Clinton's National Security Council.

As a refugee whose family fled Czechoslovakia, first from the Nazis and later from the Communists, Albright represents the highest ideals and aspirations of immigrants who come to America seeking to make major contributions to our society. As a leader in international relations, she has helped change the course of history and, in so doing, has also set a new standard for American women and for women around the world.

After leaving the Secretary of State post in 2001, she authored several bestsellers, launched a private investment fund, and provided global strategy consulting. In 2012, she received the Presidential Medal of Freedom.

Influence on American Diplomacy

As Secretary of State, Albright promoted the expansion of NATO eastward into the former Soviet bloc nations and the non-proliferation of nuclear weapons from the former Soviet republics to rogue nations, successfully pressed for military intervention under NATO auspices during the humanitarian crisis in Kosovo in 1999, supported the expansion of free-market democratization and the creation of civil societies in the developing world, favored the ratification of the Kyoto Protocol on Global Climate Change, and furthered the normalization of relations with Vietnam.

Nancy Pelosi

Nancy Pelosi was the 52nd Speaker of the House of Representatives, having made history in 2007 when she was elected the first woman to serve as Speaker of the House, and in her third term as Speaker, Pelosi made history again in January 2019 when she regained her position second-in-line to the presidency, the first person to do so in more than 60 years. As Speaker, Pelosi was fighting For The People, working to lower health care costs, increase workers' pay through strong

economic growth and rebuilding America, and clean up corruption to make Washington work for all.

For 33 years, Speaker Pelosi has represented San Francisco, California's 12th District, in Congress. She has led House Democrats for 16 years and served as House Democratic Whip. In 2013, she was inducted into the National Women's Hall of Fame at a ceremony in Seneca Falls, the birthplace of the American women's rights movement.

Under the leadership of Pelosi, the 111th Congress was heralded as "one of the most productive Congresses in history" by Congressional scholar Norman Ornstein. President Barack Obama called Speaker Pelosi "an extraordinary leader for the American people," and the Christian Science Monitor wrote: "…make no mistake: Nancy Pelosi is the most powerful woman in American politics and the most powerful House Speaker since Sam Rayburn a half century ago."

Working in partnership with President Obama, Speaker Pelosi led House passage of the American Recovery and Reinvestment Act in early 2009 to create and save millions of American jobs, provide relief for American families, and provide a tax cut to 95 percent of working Americans. With the House Democratic Caucus, Pelosi continued to focus on the need to create jobs in America and prevented them from being shipped overseas.

Former Speaker Pelosi was the architect of the landmark Affordable Care Act which has guaranteed protections for all

Americans with pre-existing medical conditions, ended annual and lifetime limits on health coverage, and provided affordable health coverage for tens of millions more Americans while lowering health care costs over the long term.

Pelosi has also made the climate crisis her flagship issue, enacting comprehensive energy legislation in 2007 that raised vehicle fuel efficiency standards for the first time in 32 years and making an historic commitment to American home grown biofuels. In 2009, under her leadership, the House passed the landmark American Clean Energy and Security Act – a comprehensive bill to create clean energy jobs, combat the climate crisis, and transition America to a clean energy economy. The legislation was blocked by Republicans in the United States Senate, but sent a strong signal to the world about the United States' commitment to fighting the climate crisis.

A leader on the environment at home and abroad, Pelosi secured passage of the "Pelosi amendment" in 1989, now a global tool to assess the potential environmental impacts of development. In San Francisco, Pelosi was the architect of legislation to create the Presidio Trust and transform the former military post into an urban national park.

In continuing to push for accountability and transparency in government, under Speaker Pelosi, the House passed the toughest ethics reform legislation in the history of the Congress, including the creation of an independent ethics panel, and increased accountability and transparency in House operations, including earmark reforms. As Speaker, Pelosi led

the fight to pass the DISCLOSE Act in the House, which fights a corporate takeover of U.S. elections and ensured additional disclosure.

Additional key accomplishments signed into law under the leadership of Speaker Pelosi include: an increase in the minimum wage for the first time in 10 years; the largest college aid expansion since the GI bill; a new GI education bill for veterans of the Iraq and Afghanistan wars; and increased services for veterans, caregivers, and the Veterans Administration.

As House Democratic Leader, Pelosi wrested critical legislative victories out of the GOP majority. In the 114th Congress, she spearheaded a historic bipartisan agreement to strengthen Medicare, ending the cycle of expensive "Doc Fix" patches and transitioning away from a volume-based system toward one that rewards value, ensures the accuracy of payments and improves the quality of care. Following the Iran Nuclear Agreement, Leader Pelosi orchestrated the effort that secured the votes to uphold a possible Presidential veto of Republicans' effort to disapprove the Joint Comprehensive Plan of Action.

In the face of the all out-Republican onslaught against Americans' health care, Leader Pelosi held House Democrats united through dozens of votes to repeal or undermine the Affordable Care Act – mobilizing a massive nationwide campaign to block House Republicans' monstrous "Trumpcare" legislation. Under her leadership, House Democrats also unanimously opposed the GOP tax fraud for the rich.

Hillary Clinton

The American presidential election of 2016 almost contributed a woman president to the global women's movement, feminism activists, women's rights networks and the agents of political feminism all around the world. Hillary Clinton came forward as the first woman presidential candidate of a major party and pursued a feminist friendly campaign. In that sense, she was a great hope for the future of feminist politics in terms of women's participation in electoral politics –particularly office holding. A woman president governing one of the hegemonic powers of the international system such as the United States (US) was a historic chance for women's attempts at claiming politics. To incorporate the neglected experiences and discourses of women into the mainstream practices of high and low politics by a feminist American president would have repercussions not only for the US, but the rest of the world as well. Low politics, which are the issue areas not inevitable for the survival of the state, are more open to women's participation. High politics with issue areas such as foreign policy and security are more directly related to the survival of the state and generally exclude women, their discourse and values from the policy-making procedures. A woman president would have integrated both the high and the low politics in the way to make feminism influential even, or especially, in matters of survival.

Upon her graduation from Yale Law School, she first worked for Children's Defense Fund in Cambridge, Massachusetts,

and then joined the team advising the Judiciary Committee of the House of Representatives on Nixon's impeachment subsequent to the Watergate Scandal. One of her opinion pieces from 1974 would later be blamed for promoting radical feminism by the Republican Patrick Buchanan on the grounds of its defending "the ability of children to sue their parents." Clinton's appearance on the political scene as First Lady took place in 1992, which was the UN's Year of the Woman. Her contribution to the 1995 Fourth World Congress on Women in Beijing with the words "Human rights are women's rights, and women's rights are human rights" became a monumental moment in the history of women's rights. Hillary Clinton would, twenty years later, announce that her 2016 candidacy was intended to finally launch the 12-part plan for women's empowerment she had proposed in Beijing. Nevertheless, she is also known to have voted for the Patriot Act in 2001, the authorization of the Iraq War in 2002, and the Wall Street bailout in 2008; none was compatible with the ethical feminist standpoint. However, she later admitted that her Iraq vote as a senator was a mistake.

Much of Clinton's early work in the Senate focused on promoting economic development in upstate New York—including the expansion of high-speed Internet access and the creation of tax incentives for environmentally friendly building projects. She also promoted programs to renovate and modernize schools. After the September 11, 2001, terrorist attacks on the World Trade Center in New York City, she worked to help the region recover. Because of the attacks, New York lost one-third of all its office space in Lower Manhattan; key rail and subway lines closed, displacing more than a half

million commuters; and tens of thousands of jobs were lost. Clinton worked with her colleagues to ensure New York received federal funds to begin rebuilding. She fought to include $50 million for New York area nonprofits and $570 million in infrastructure security in 2004. Eventually, more than $21.4 billion was appropriated to rebuild and secure the city and affected areas. Clinton also won an extension of unemployment insurance to help displaced workers.

During her time in the Senate, Clinton was either in the minority party or part of a razor-thin majority. While a few of her standalone bills became law, Clinton focused on policy work in committee and on establishing bipartisan relationships. Virginia Senator John William Warner, the Republican chair of the Armed Services Committee, praised Clinton's efforts. "She's very industrious," he said. "She does her homework very carefully. She's very respectful of how the committee does its business."

Condoleezza Rice

Condoleezza Rice, born on November 14, 1954, is an American diplomat and political scientist. As a senior advisor to President George H.W. Bush and as a National Security Advisor and 66th Secretary of State under President George W. Bush, Dr. Rice had a unique vantage point, helping to craft American foreign policy.

She became a germination point for Bush foreign policy, from the war in Iraq to sidelining Yasir Arafat to the policy of

preemption. As a Russia specialist and a former provost of Stanford University, she melded her realism--the view that great powers act in their own self-interest--with what she called Mr. Bush's idealism, or what his critics said his naïve belief in a "moral" American foreign policy that can spread democracy throughout the world. In this equation, Ms. Rice was the unsentimental academic who focused on facts and history, while Mr. Bush started with a set of big-picture principles rooted in his Christian faith, along with a politician's sense about other leaders and the pressures that drive them. Ms. Rice said that she saw her job as translating the president's instincts into policy, and that he influenced her as much as she influenced him.

Along with Mr. Powell, Ms. Rice urged Mr. Bush to intervene militarily in the civil war in Liberia, over the opposition of the Pentagon. Mr. Bush eventually approved sending a contingent of two hundred marines.

In Northern Ireland, Mr. Bush and Ms. Rice had a tense disagreement about a phrase that Mr. Bush planned to use in a joint news conference with Prime Minister Tony Blair of Britain. With American and British forces making quick gains in Iraq, Mr. Bush wanted to say that the United Nations would have a "vital role" in an American-led occupation. Mr. Blair and Mr. Powell agreed. But Ms. Rice, according to a senior administration official, was under pressure from officials who disliked the United Nations and thought "vital" was going too far.

The president used the word anyway--not once, but nine times. Afterward, the senior administration official said, Ms. Rice was "fussing about it a bit because she was afraid she might have some explaining to do back here in order to cover all of our various constituencies. And after a while, the president got annoyed about it."

As a Secretary of State, Rice pioneered the policy of Transformational Diplomacy directed toward expanding the number of responsible democratic governments in the world and especially in the Greater Middle East. Rice stated that the September 11 attacks in 2001 were rooted in "oppression and despair" and so, the U.S. must advance democratic reform and support basic rights throughout the greater Middle East.

As Secretary of State, Rice traveled heavily and initiated many diplomatic efforts on behalf of the Bush administration; she holds the record for most miles logged in the position. Her diplomacy relied on strong presidential support and is considered to be the continuation of style defined by former Republican secretaries of state Henry Kissinger and James Baker.

Rice was a proponent of the 2003 invasion of Iraq. After Iraq delivered its declaration of weapons of mass destruction to the United Nations on December 8, 2002, Rice wrote an editorial for The New York Times entitled "Why We Know Iraq Is Lying". In a January 10, 2003, interview with CNN's Wolf Blitzer, Rice made headlines by stating regarding Iraqi president Saddam Hussein's nuclear capabilities: "The problem here is that there will always be some uncertainty about how

quickly he can acquire nuclear weapons. But we don't want the smoking gun to be a mushroom cloud."

When asked about the many threats around the world today – such as Syria, North Korea, and ISIS – Dr. Rice instead pointed to a broader threat that links many of the challenges we face, what she termed a crisis of confidence in a functioning world order. She noted that the architecture that America devised and maintained in the seven decades since the end of World War II – including political, military, and economic structures – is being neglected and at risk of collapse.

After the end of the Bush Administration, Rice returned to academia and joined the Council on Foreign Relations.

Michelle Obama

"Since stepping reluctantly into public life, I've been held up as the most powerful woman in the world and taken down as an "angry black woman."

I've wanted to ask my detractors which part of that phrase matters to them the most—is it "angry" or "black" or "woman"? I've smiled for photos with people who call my husband horrible names on national television, but still want a framed keepsake for their mantel. I've heard about the swampy parts of the internet that question everything about me, right down to whether I'm a woman or a man. A sitting U.S. congressman has made fun of my butt. I've been hurt. I've

been furious. But mostly, I've tried to laugh this stuff off." –
Michelle Obama in her memoir, Becoming

In Becoming – the first book that tells Michelle Obama's story
from her own perspective – she reveals that her life is a form
of alchemy. Her childhood, growing up on the South Side of
Chicago, is recalled with an essentially American kind of
wholesomeness: a strong nuclear family of four, sharing a one-
bed apartment upstairs while the one below was occupied by
her piano teacher great aunt Robbie. Her family worked hard
and kept things moving upwards.

She describes herself in her early years as "the striver". Later,
campaigning for the first time with her husband, she recounts
the moment she realized that her task is mainly to share this
story with "people who despite the difference in skin color
reminded me of my family – postal workers who had bigger
dreams just as her grandfather Dandy once had; civic-minded
piano teachers like Robbie; stay-at-home moms who were
active in the PTA like my mother; blue-collar workers who'd
do anything for their families, just like my dad. I didn't need to
practice or use notes. I said only what I sincerely felt."

Girl from the South Side and former First Lady. Wife, mother,
dog lover." This is how Michelle Obama describes herself.
Although she is surely most known for her role and work as
the former First Lady and wife of the 44th President Barack
Obama, Michelle will most certainly have her own legacy,
separate from her husband's. And it will be that she was the
first First Lady to show women that it is ok to be everything

and that all women deserve equal opportunity and choice, every and any choice.

Raised on the South Side of Chicago, Michelle describes her upbringing as conventional. Dad worked, mom stayed at home raising her and her brother and they ate dinner together each night at the dining table. Every daughter wants to please their father (or most anyway), but Michelle had an extra strong desire to do so given her father's health struggles with MS. So, his desire for her to stay out of trouble and be a good student greatly impacted her growing up and she was determined to meet and exceed his expectations.

With a B.A. from Princeton University followed by a J.D. from Harvard Law School and her many social and community focused accomplishments since, it goes without saying that her father, who passed away in 1991, would be more than proud!

Michelle spent her early legal career working at the law firm Sidley Austin, where she met her husband. She subsequently worked as the Associate Dean of Student Services at the University of Chicago and the Vice President for Community and External Affairs of the University of Chicago Medical Center.

In 1992, Barack and Michelle married and as we all know they have two lovely daughters, Malia and Sasha. Michelle campaigned for her husband's presidential bid throughout 2007 and 2008 and then became the First Lady!

As First Lady, Michelle became a role model for women, a fashion icon, and an advocate for education, poverty awareness, healthy eating and physical activity.

In a fast-paced, hectic life filled with accomplishment and meaning, the first African American former first lady of the United States, Michelle Obama has appeared as one of the most compelling and iconic women of our era. Her insightful, intimate, inspiring memoir reveals her as an influential and powerful woman since she served as a role model for many people in the world with her words, actions, and legacy.

The first African American lady of the United States to serve in that role. Michelle created the most inclusive and welcoming in the White House's history, while also being a powerful advocate for education for children around the world, girls and women in the United States, raised awareness of the importance to pursue healthier lives for families, spoke up about gender equality and provided a glimpse of her husband Barack Obama with his leadership qualities as a powerful leader with his highest repute across America.

Along the way, she aced Carpool Karaoke, showed us a few dance moves, and lived life under the glare of publicity. From sitting down with Oprah and doing push-ups with Ellen DeGeneres, she's a woman full of positivity, warmth, and strength in an era that shaped her as a role model for our generation.

Michelle herself, humbly mentioned that she is just an ordinary woman who has lived an extraordinary life. Michelle Obama

said in Becoming, "In sharing my story, I hope to help create space for other stories and other voices, to widen the pathway for who belongs and why."

Through her admirable qualities, courageous action, mesmerizing storytelling, and work deep of reflection, Michelle Obama recounts the experiences that have shaped her with insight, motherhood, and to her time spent at Chicago's South Side to the White House. With lively wit and unerring honesty, Michelle explains her disappointments and her triumphs, both private and public, on her own terms and in her own words – telling her entire story as she has lived it.

As a truly modern-day, revolutionary woman, who has championed a multitude of important causes throughout her life, she has encouraged better education for girls, equal rights, healthy living and more help for families living in poverty.

In 2010, as First Lady, Michelle launched her Let's Move initiative, aimed at addressing the childhood obesity problem gripping the United States. She urged kids to make healthy choices and campaigned for companies and schools to offer healthier eating options.

Michelle focused on education in 2014, inspiring children to succeed academically. She used her own upbringing to show what this could achieve, telling supporters of her Reach Higher initiative, "I am an example of what is possible when girls, from the very beginning of their lives, are loved and nurtured by people around them."

She urged young people to continue their education beyond high school, giving themselves the tools to decide how to pursue their chosen path to the best of their abilities.

In 2015, she and Barack Obama launched Let Girls Learn, encouraging girls to stay in school and asking the government to make a greater investment in their education. "No country can ever truly flourish if it stifles the potential of its women and deprives itself of the contributions of half its citizens," she said.

Appealing directly to girls and young women, Michelle told them, "You don't want to be with a boy who is too stupid to appreciate a smart young lady. There is no boy who is cute enough, or interesting enough, to stop you from getting your education."

In his presidential farewell address, her husband publicly described Michelle as having done everything with "grace, grit, style and good humor." Everything she does is done with passion, from breaking down stereotypes to removing the barriers for girls' education.

Michelle Obama encourages us not to give up. We mustn't be cynical. We must live life with purpose, and maximize our human potential with optimism because, in the end, we should always believe things that are possible, then we become.

Kamala Harris

Kamala Devi Harris is an American politician and attorney who is the 49th and current vice president of the United States. She is the first female vice president and the highest-ranking female official in U.S. history, as well as the first African American and first Asian American vice president. A member of the Democratic Party, she previously served as the attorney general of California from 2011 to 2017 and as a United States senator representing California from 2017 to 2021.

For countless women and girls, Harris' achievement of reaching the second highest office in the country represents hope, validation and the shattering of a proverbial glass ceiling that has kept mostly white men perched at the top tiers of American government.

"She's literally the blueprint to women's political possibility and now she is stepping literally into the Oval Office and she's going to put an intersectional lens on everything this administration does from a gender or race lens," said Glynda Carr, the president and CEO of Higher Heights, which focuses on electing Black women into political offices.

Harris, a 56-year-old California senator who is the first Black woman and the first person of South Asian descent elected to the vice presidency, has long credited civil rights legends like Shirley Chisholm, Mary McLeod Bethune and Fannie Lou Hamer as sources of inspiration, as well as her Indian mother, Shyamala Gopalan.

She paid tribute to the women, particularly Black women, who paved the way for her. "While I may be the first woman in this office, I will not be the last," Harris said in her first post-election address to the nation.

Los Angeles mother Kim Rincon sat with her arm around her 9-year-old daughter, Jordan, to watch the speech. A year ago, Rincon and Jordan had met Harris backstage at a rally during her bid for president in the 2020 Democratic primaries. Jordan gave Harris the "Kamala for President" button she was wearing before Harris crouched to the ground to thank her at eye level.

"Harris was being celebrated as this superstar at that rally and now on stage accepting the vice presidency," said Rincon, whose daughter is Mexican and Vietnamese American. "My biggest hope is that Jordan grows up thinking this is normal."

Her tireless work ethic, unapologetic ambition and desire to serve are among the reasons President Joe Biden selected her his running mate. And as is the case with many strong women, she is the product of a loving family, led by a powerful mother.

Harris speaks often of her late mom, Shyamala Gopalan Harris, Ph.D. She referred to her during remarks in Delaware while announcing the appointment of top science advisers in the new Biden administration.

"I feel a certain kinship with the nominees we are bringing together today," said Harris. "Because my mother was a scientist, an endocrinologist. She was passionate about science,

and basically had two goals in her life: To raise her two daughters, and to end breast cancer."

Harris noted that when she was young, she would accompany her mother to the lab, where she'd be given jobs to do. "And when you're the daughter of a scientist, science has a way of shaping how you think and see the world. My mother used to talk about the scientific method as if it were a way of life. And she instilled in me a fundamental belief in the importance of collecting and analyzing data. Facts."

Harris has long been a champion for equality and a critic of any form of discrimination based on age, race, sex, religion, sexual orientation and gender identity. Whenever one speaks with Harris, there is a sense that people are important.

Harris often encourages and recognizes other women. In her VP acceptance speech in November, she shouted out Black women and other women of color. And during a science advisers announcement, Harris noted the Biden administration, "will make sure we are investing in STEM education and the next generation of scientists, including women scientists and scientists of color."

She spoke proudly of the "world-renowned scientists and distinguished experts" who are joining the administration and shouted out a sister scientist.

"A few weeks ago, I got the first dose of my coronavirus vaccine," said Harris. "It was the Moderna vaccine, and it was developed with the National Institutes of Health by a team that was co-led by a 34-year-old Black woman named Dr.

Kizzmekia Corbett." Harris continued: "I have a message for all the little girls and boys out there, who dream of growing up to be superheroes. Superheroes aren't just figments of our imagination," she said. "They're walking among us. They're teachers, doctors and scientists. …And you can grow up to be like them, too."

Harris closed that day with this: "So, dream big, lead with conviction, and see yourselves as the superheroes of tomorrow—because that's who you are. See yourselves that way and pursue your dreams, not only for your sake, but for ours. Our country needs you."

Women can be said to be the founders of 21st-century politics. They have broken the sexism and racism barriers which no longer take a center-stage in American politics. The rise of Sen. Kamala Harris to the office of the Vice President, hundreds of women vying for different seats in the Senate and House, and millions others who vote as a bloc, is a clear testament that women have arrived—and they are here to stay. The American political dream is no longer out of reach for women.. prevent

Madeleine Jana Korbel Albright
Former United States Secretary of State

Nancy Pelosi
The former speaker of the United States House of
Representative.

Hillary Clinto
The former United States Secretary of State.

Condoleezza Rice
Former United States Secretary of State

Michelle Obama
The former First Lady of the United States

Kamala Harris
Vice President of the United States

Chapter 5:
THE FORGOTTEN HEROINES OF SOUTH SUDAN

"Strong women aren't simply born. They are forged through the challenges of life. With each challenge, they grow mentally and emotionally. They move forward with their head held high and a strength that cannot be denied. A woman who's been through the storm and survived. Women are warriors!"—Anonymous.

Long before and during the European colonization of Africa, ancient kingdoms and empires thrived for centuries on the continent. Some were headed by women, including female warriors who led armies against invading European powers to defend their people from conquest and enslavement. Even though women have been at the forefront of impressive exploits in combat, their stories are often overlooked and forgotten. In this chapter, I intend to remind ourselves about the women who have fought in the front line and played active roles in liberating their people from oppression and armed conflicts especially in South Sudan side by side with men. There is a need to tell the forgotten history

113

of South Sudanese women and from across the world who have played a critical role in the liberation struggle for independence of their countries in particular and the world at large—the women of the world.

In South Sudan, just like the case worldwide, many female warriors have been forgotten in the patriarchal culture and institutions that consider women as less equal to men. There is a lot of weirdness in this world where people are less to think through, seriously constrained by social construction. It is important to consider social construction as part of our lives but also as part of indoctrinating individuals.

There is a need to keep updating our traditions in a way that fits the striving for progress, there is a need to consider substantial issues regarding policies put forward that put traditions that pressurize female children into lower statuses than male children. In that regard, this chapter shall contribute to efforts that are put in place to uplift women. A young girl needs to have a historical role model to strive forward. Besides, the world is a social structure with the transcendent ground in which the world's institution named state is standing. All humans need to understand the historical background of our initial experience. The concept of women and men is not only based on biological differences but also the social activities.

Historical background of South Sudan state

To understand the state's structures that were undermining the women's situation, one has to study what had happened in Sudan in the past. South Sudan has a long history of struggle

from ancient Kush to modern Sudan. Before colonization, Sudan was a territory of separate independent entities. It was a vast land rich in diverse cultures which were named by foreigners as Bilaat El Soud or the Land of Black.

It was not until the Neolithic Revolution that men began to take more and more control over human society. The rise of some religions, especially the Prophet Mohammed in sixth century A.D, also gave rise to Mahdi State in Sudan. Such structures of institutions that favor men were inherited by Sudan with the rise of Sudanization.

The concept of Sudanization is the idea that Sudan started at one point and that it was not there before the rise of Arabs' Prophet Mohammed. At that period, the structures that were setup were taking ground not only in Sudan but in different parts of the world. Sudan and South Sudan of today were one state with Islamic institutions which started with the rise of Sudan's Mahdiyya State.

For sure, we can't deny the role of the institution in shaping people's behaviors. Sudan and South Sudan were previous institutions established by religious successive regimes. The first institution that undermines women's role and shaping of their personalities is a family. Family upbringing has a greater role in the making of state's institutions. Nonetheless, the State as an important institution has played a crucial part in undermining women's role in human society.

However, there were several regimes of foreign forces whose aims were to gain resources and Manpower. Such foreign

forces never establish institutions with policies that consider women. For example, modern history of Sudan involved several parties including foreign forces like Mohammed Ali Pasha's invasion of Sudan in 1821. The Turco-Egyptian era has no political and state structure because Mohammed Ali as a Commander did not establish institutions. He did establish slave centers called Zeiriba and recruited people to his army. It was some kind of anarchy which made the Nation not able to design policies that support women participation.

Before the region became Sudan, there were several states namely Darfur State in the West, Soba State in the Central, Punj Kingdom in the East, and the Nuer State and other Kingdoms in the South. Sudanization was on the rise with the emergence of the Turco-Egyptians invasion of North Sudan. That caused the fall of all states in the North which eventually included the South under one single territory and state which became known as Sudan State. As a result, in 1956, Sudan got its independence from Anglo-Egyptians condominium but the region of Southern Sudan remained marginalized. That caused another civil war between the north predominated by Muslim Arabs and the South with the majority of Christians. The war started before independence in 1955 which continued until 1972 when the Addis Ababa Peace Agreement was signed. After three years of agreement in 1975, a mutiny against the government led by Kuany Latjor started in a little town called Bilkay (known as Akoba). That mutiny led to the establishment of a military camp which became known later as Bilpam. That small rebel group that was calling for the independence of South Sudan took nine years fighting the government before the establishment of SPLM later in 1984. However, Sudan

never experienced nationalism due to distinct cultures. These diverse cultures were also divided along religious lines: Islam and Christianity. These distinctive religions and traditions brought institutions that are unfriendly to girls and women. That is why understanding the political structures of successive regimes is important to know the condition of women in Sudan and South Sudan.

The Country went through several stages of struggle where people were not only suffering from wars, death, hunger, and diseases, but also against the axiomatic structure of political institutions which has its root in the culture itself. The wars were against injustice and also against the indoctrination of cultural ideologies and religions that design policies that are not inclusive.

Women have participated in these wars in many different ways. They have made an insurmountable contribution during the liberation struggle to the birth of their nation. Those on the battlefield and those who had dedicated their service through running humanitarian aid in the war-torn region.

From 1955 to 2005, many Anya Nya 1 soldiers, Anya Nya 2, and SPLA soldiers relied on the southern Sudan civil populations for food and accommodation. The women played an active role in political mobilizations; preparing food and clean water; carrying ammunition; doing laundry for the troops and offering other humanitarian services such as volunteering as nurses. Others remained home to take care of their families while their husbands were deployed on various front lines across South Sudan.

One of the noticeable heroines among the bravest women of South Sudan who helped their male counterparts run the war as they embarked on political mobilization and improving mechanisms to feed the soldiers at the battleground was Emma McCune, the late wife of Dr. Riek Machar.

Emma was an expatriate British foreign aid worker in Sudan. Before meeting and later on marrying the Southern rebel leader Dr. Riek Machar, the current First Vice President of South Sudan. Emma used her position at an NGO to help the women and the children in South Sudan. Through Unicef a Canadian, funded humanitarian organization.

The organization re-opened a lot of village schools in the country's south during the war. She also delivered food, provided shelter and medicines. Emma was a champion of children's rights and she rescued more than 150 child soldiers.

Women on the frontline

For some women, working as nurses and offering other humanitarian services was not enough. Several women enlisted and fought alongside their male counterparts as foot soldiers. They fought for many of the same reasons as men did: out of a sense of patriotism; to liberate their beloved country.

Some women joined the men in receiving military training such as "Katiba Bannat" or "Girls battalion". Katiba Bannat were great warriors and fearless women in the face of cannons from the enemy side. They fought harder to defend their country.

During that time the leadership of SPLM sent a good number of women and girls to Cuba and other countries for specialized training especially in the medical field, and other humanitarian services.

Some of the heroines who took active part in the front line during the civil wars were the late Captain Nyanyaak Puoch Mar Wang, the late Captain Nyanyaak Dhuording Choul, Nyaulang Reat Chany, Aker Garang, and Satona. Captain Nyanaak Puoch was a chairlady for the Women Association in SPLM liberation areas. The purpose of the women's association was to mobilize women to join the military. As a result, women participated in the liberation of the border town of Jokow. Jokow is a town at the border of Ethiopia and Sudan. They also liberated other areas in the South. Among those women who played significant roles was Nyawang Beliu who completed her training in 1985-1986 to participate in physical fighting at Jokow as well as with Katiba Bannat.

Women like Nyanguok Riek and her team played a very important role as well. They were very active in preparing food and clean water and other needs to help the soldiers.

Some women lost their lives as martyrs on the battlefields of South Sudan. We owe them the living debt of our dignity and the glory that many South Sudanese enjoy. South Sudan is like any other Country worldwide where women stand tall in the liberation struggle for liberty and freedom of their nations. These were living heroes to young boys and girls. The role of women in South Sudan's struggle was very clear in all ways.

119

If we look at world history we can even say that the first human struggle started by women's struggle in pregnancy, nursing a baby after delivery to survive is considered as the first struggle. Women's struggle is everlasting as it is always there for humanity to continue to progress. History-making is bitter, painful, and not easy from all sides, the woman who took Guns is also a Mother who bears the pain of the death of her husband and taking care of the orphans. Women of South Sudan have suffered a lot during the war for independence,

The liberation struggle was heavily on mothers and women in general. Most have fallen upon women's shoulders alongside people in uniforms. No Men were standing alone at the front line without women throughout the history of humanity. Historians always seem to forget the undeniable role of women in politics, struggle, and wars, simply because their memories were preoccupied with axiomatic structures that were inherited from previous states. That axiomatic line of thinking has historical roots in successive regimes.

Historical root and the nature of women participation

There was a huge historical axiomatic system that prevented women from participating in the politics of Sudan and South Sudan. Guess what? The current political structure of Sudan started by the Turco-Egyptians regime of 1821-1825 (1) (2) (3) (4), followed by the reign of Khedive Ismail 1863-1881, the new regime that succeeded the Khedive regime has followed the same route as the First ruler. After the reign of Khedive, came the Madhist state which lasted for 17 years from 1881-to

1898. And the Anglo-Egyptian condominium in 1899-1955, which has lasted 57 years.

Through all these years, there was a historical structure of the traditional state that has lasted many years that suppressed Women's role in politics and economic decisions. This brought about the historical, social, and political structure which consolidated the status quo of women in history. It is a historical structure because it has a culture that becomes axiomatic to the mental orientation of young kids both girls and Boys. The areas that were traditionalized by such a traditional state were political decision making which includes educational, social, and economic. Successive regimes were produced by such social tradition iterated from the past which taught children that way. The tradition is rooted in Islamic religion and African cultures. Within that axiomatic structure represented by (5), religious families of Mirghani and Mahdiyya in the North and African practice in the South had influenced how to understand our history.

Such a state had facilitated a patriarchal society which became the builder of Sudan's modern state. British rule in the North that started in 1890 and subsequently the whole of Sudan until 1947 did not change much of that tradition. There was no space for women in both Mirghania and Mahdiyya's political structure while the political structure in the South was not stable because there was no single institution established. That condition had made the situation in the South completely different from that of North Sudan because of the anarchy of civil war that prevented the institutionalization of Islamic law in the South. There was no problem recruiting Girls into the

new rebel movement established in the South. The political institutions in the South were not as effective as they were in North Sudan. The only institution that was admired by Southerners was a rebel institution that was not officially recognized and whose focus was on the liberation struggle. Women were participating in a military whose leaders were Men. As a result of that situation, there was no time to think about girls' education nor institutional policies that call for girls' rights. Now, there is a need to consider issues that were not addressed in the past including women's right to participate in politics and the building of institutions. There were structured institutions in Sudan that put men at the high level of the state's leadership. These institutions were structured by successive regimes of Mahdiyya and Merghaniyya as I mentioned earlier. These types of regimes were there consistently until 2005. With CPA, South Sudan became an independent state on 9 July 2011 with the hope for a new dawn but civil war erupted because of rampant corruption and ethnicity.

The Forgotten Heroines of South Sudan

The South Sudanese women played important roles during the first liberation struggle that raged for almost seventeen years (1955 -1972), both at home and in uniform. Not only did they give their sons, husbands, fathers, and brothers to the war effort, they gave their time, energy, and some even gave their lives. Some of these uncelebrated heroines who played active roles in Anyanya I Civil War between North and South of the Sudan include Sergeant Nyakang, Corporal Nyadut, Nyadol, Ager Gum, Nyawec Kay, Nyanbol Garang and Nyayey Chuc

(wife to late commander John Kong Nyuon), Comrades Nyakang and Nyadol who hail from Lou Nuer of Akobo from Jonglei State, Comrade Nyawec Kay from a section of Dok Nuer of Leer County, and Nyadut from Nyuong Nuer, Panyijar in Unity State.

These brave women were not only supporting fighters, but they were also combatants themselves. They rose up the ranks in the army, commanded soldiers and fought fierce battles. After the war, they were integrated into Sudan Armed Forces and various organized forces such as police, prison services, wildlife and civil defense services (commonly known as fire brigade). They underwent military training and emerged as brave fighters. After completion of training and military orientation, they were deployed to different regions in Sudan. Sergeant Nyakang was deployed to Nasir and Nyadol deployed to Malakal, the capital city of Upper Nile State. Ager Gum was also integrated into the police services and deployed in Rumbek, Lake State in the Greater region of Bahr El Ghazal. When the war erupted again in Bor in 1983, which culminated in the formation of Sudan People's Liberation Movement and Army (SPLM/A), Comrade Agum joined SPLM/A. She was promoted to the rank of major.

Other courageous women who led the liberation struggle from front were Comrade Sarah Nyakuoth Kuac, the widow of late Commander William Nyuon Bany, the third in command of the SPM/A liberation struggle after the late Dr. John Garang de Mabior and the late Kerbino Kuanyi Bol. Commander Nyuon was also a member of SPLM/A Military High Command. Commander William Nyuon Bany was the Chief

of General Staff of SPLM/A. It is fair to mention here that the late William Nyuon led the mutiny of Ayod/ Jonglei State one month after the Bor incident on 16th May 1983.

Comrade Sarah Nyakuoth Kuac, despite being a wife to a commander, was also a great combatant. She fought several fierce battles and won. With other combatants, they were chased to swamps (Sudd) between 1964-1965. The swampy regions became their hide-out for one-year. Their situation was dire. Apart from living in water, they lacked ammunition and guns to fight the enemy. Despite these deplorable conditions, Sarah Nyakuoth Kuay continued with the liberation struggle. Her mission never ended with Anyanya in 1972 that granted the then southern Sudan self-rule within a united Sudan. Comrade Sarah Nyakuoth rejoined the liberation struggle together with her husband, Commander William Nyuon Bany in Ayod on 15th May 1983. Sarah Nyakuoth Kuac is now a member of the Council of States (Senate), the legislative body that represents the interest of the State at a national level. It is worth noting that the youngest nation of South Sudan has a bicameral system of legislation.

Role of Women in the second liberation struggle

1983 marked the collapse of the Addis Ababa peace accord that was signed on the 3rd day of March 1972. Among several women who joined the Sudan People's Liberation Movement and Army was Mary Jok Bukjiok (currently a member of National Parliament representing Fangak County). Being a teenager serving the rebels, the more she listened to political myths, the more she became motivated and passionate to be

part of the revolution. Mary listened to revolutionary stories with eagerness. She wanted to know why they came to the bush, how Arab Muslim treated South Sudanese et cetera.

That was the attitude of those who joined the movement on the eve of its establishment in 1983. She voluntarily joined as an interpreter at the age of 16. This opportunity was availed to her at the inception of the movement in 1982 when the first group of revolutionaries spearheaded the struggle for independence of South Sudan. Her fluency in Amharic language made her act as a bridge between the new recruits and the host country - Ethiopia. Some of these liberators were Gatjiek Teny, Lokurnyang, Oyay Deng Ajak and Pag'an Amum.

Before she joined the movement, Mary studied in Ethiopia where she learned Amharic. Her knowledge of Amharic was an asset to the movement. Commander William Nyuon and other leaders made her a translator. She played an important role in connecting the movement with Ethiopians and the Nuer people; the pioneers of the movement.

Before the birth of SPLA, there was a recurrence of rebellion already existing in a place called Bilpam. The leader of that rebel movement was Benson Kuany Latjor. The rebel movement consisted of the Nuer who rebelled from Akobo in 1975. Commander Benson Kuany was the first rebel leader who established Bilpam Military camp on the Ethiopian border.

In February 1983, a man called Garjiek Wie arrived in Ethiopia
to join the movement established earlier by Benson Kuany.
Those rebels, under Benson Kuany Latjor, named themselves
the Anyanya II. They considered themselves the second
rebellion after the peace agreement. They were not satisfied
with the peace agreement signed in Addis Ababa, Ethiopia.
Along with the first group were Koang Chuol Kulang, Tap
Yoal and Chuol Deng Luoth, who had been in Bilpam since
1982.

On 7th March1983, Samuel Gai Tut arrived in Itang at the
Border of Sudan and Ethiopia. Itang was a refugee settlement
camp near Bilpam. Samuel Gai Tut was a former Anyanya I
officer, who was calling for an independent and sovereign state
to be known as the Republic of South Sudan. He was also a
former Minister of Wildlife and Tourism in the regional
government – High Executive Council. The High Executive
Council was established by the Addis Ababa Agreement which
granted South Sudanese self-attorney or self-rule. Samuel Gai's
status as a politician and senior in military command in the
then Anyanya I had an advantage to be the leader of the new
movement -Anyanya II. His colleagues honored and respected
him for profoundly being known as a man of high integrity,
fairness and equality.

Mary, as an interpreter, was helping to integrate new recruits
into the community as well as into the liberation struggle. Her
beauty, intelligence and smartness charmed the influential
leader, Commander Wiliam Nyuon Bany, who fell in love with
her. This revolutionary love with a rebel later culminated in
marriage in 1986.

Hon. Mary Jok's work was not only to translate but also to smuggle food to soldiers. Among the leaders that were not Nuer were Lokunyang Lado (Murle) and his colleagues. Mary Jok was trying to find food for them. There was a lack of food in refugee camps in Ethiopia. People survived on what they called monna (by-products or leftovers of mixed yeast and floor) for brewing local wine. To improve their food quality, Mary smuggled maize for them from local farmers.

Garjiek Wie went to Ethiopians to inform them that they want to establish a Military base in Bilpam. At regional politics of East Africa – the Intergovernmental Authority on Development (IGAD), Ethiopia was not happy with Sudan because they were supporting separatist in the northern part of Ethiopia - Eritrea. Ethiopia wanted to use rebels from Sudan to pressurize the Sudanese government to stop their support for Eretria. The Ethiopian government responded to Garjiek Wie's request by sending food to Itang using River Boat from Gambella regional capital. Following the arrival of Samuel Gai Tut, the second group that followed were Comrade Gen. Oyay Deng Ajak, Comrade Isaac Tut Dhoyier, Comrade Pagan Amum Okech, Comrade Rout Nyamuon and Comrade Lokurnyang Lado.

For women to contribute more effectively, they established an association which was known as the Nine Members Committee (NMC) exclusively for women. The Nine Members Committee was led by Comrade Fatma Nyawang Beliu, who is currently a member of the National Legislative Assembly in South Sudan. She was the first leader of the Women

Association. Comrade Alekiir Malual Aguer was nominated as the secretary of the Association. Comrade Nyanyak Puoch Mar, Comrade Mary Jok's Mother and Comrade Nyadeng Kerbino Kuanyin were assigned to take care of patients wounded in the war. They were responsible for nursing them. It was traumatizing work to do. Comrade Nyanyak Puoch had served for both the Nine Members Committee and 15 Members Committees.

On the other hand, among women who participated in caring for the wounded soldiers were Comrade Yar Jok, a wife to Comrade Michael Makuei Lueth the current Minister of Information and Postal Services, and Comrade Yar Poil, wife to Commander Manyal Kueth. Nyarieka Chuol was a leader of Tiaktiak battalion. Comrade Nyarieka chuol was a wife to late commander Elijah Hon Top.

Panyagor, Baidit and Mageri (1993-1995)

1983-1999 was the hardest period but worse was coming. Mary became a full-time fighter and housewife at the same time. She was among the women who cooked for the army at several warfronts. Sometimes, they prepared food and took it to the frontline. They would occasionally participate in a battle and cook afterwards. They had to cook. It was their obligation to do so.

Mary shared her difficult time as a female rebel. The worst and the longest journey she experienced was in 1993, when she walked from Lou Nuer land (Greater Akobo), in Upper Nile region to Equotoria region. Before they could reach Panyagor,

they were ambushed in Duk Padiet all the way to Magerri in Central Equotoria State. They fought at Panyagor for two days and ambushed in Dachuak and again at Baidit. The war was fought in a swampy area. The water level was extremely high. It was really hard because death was imminent. You would speak to a comrade one minute, the next minute they are gone. The scenes were horrific. Mary couldn't believe her eyes. Crossing over dead bodies of young people lined-up along the road was freezing. She remained strong in the midst of adversity and served food. It took them some months to get used to it. Death had become normal after some time on the road. Nobody knew they could reach their destination. It was difficult to go back and not easy to go forward.

War became part and parcel of their daily life. They got acquainted with war. Battle after battle. Every week people faced new battles or ambushes. Things got worse when they faced Bombardment in April 1995 at Magerri. This time, bombardment came from the real enemy- the Sudanese Army using Antonov fighter jets. Bombardment continued until they reached the village called Lafon. With Commander William Nyuon's strategies, they were able to capture the whole Arabs army including senior officers at Lafon. That angered and annoyed the Sudan Armed Forces. As a result, the Sudan Army launched a suicide attack on the rebel forces and captured two tanks at Lopit and Lowiy.

Chicken became their watchdogs. They would react to their distress call. When chickens sense danger, they make distress calls. The rebels used their sounds as signals of a looming danger. They knew that Antonov was coming to bomb the camp. They walked far away from Central Equotoria State up-to Kenyan border to the east. The distance between Magerri to

Lafon is eighteen (18) hours for men and twenty (20) hours for women.

Operations that Mary took part in (1986-1993)

Mary visited Kurmuk for three months and stayed in Yabuth, Blue Nile region of Sudan for one year. She also visited Equotoria region to participate in several battles. The operation of Equotoria region around Juba was hard enough but worse was when their army was on the move.

Mary and her comrades had to walk long distances without food. They traversed Upper Nile all the way to Equotoria. It took months to reach Equotoria region on foot and in water. Soldiers were not just moving but calculating each move through information from spies and their agents.

The ground was completely covered in flood water which made it difficult to move around. Rebels do not have homes. They have to walk from place to place. The enemy was monitoring them with frequent bombardments. As bombardment continued, people stayed in trenches for weeks or more.

Late capitan Nyanyaak Dhorading Chuol.

Captain Nyanyaak Dhorading Chuol was also a chairlady for women association in SPLM, and was well known for her excellent contribution during the liberation struggle

Hon. Angelina Nyanden Kerbino

MP/Deputy Chairperson on Humanitarian Affairs & Disaster Management.

Emma McCune Machar
Emma was an expatriate British foreign aid worker in Sudan who married Riek Machar. She was one of the bravest women of South Sudan.

Hon. Mary Jock Bukjiok
She is a member of Reconstituted Transitional National Legislative Assembly
(TNLA) representing Fangak County, Jonglei State.
She is also Deputy Chairperson of the Women Parliamentary Caucus.

133

Comrade Nyanguok Riek
Former president of Nuer community in America

Hon. Fatima Nyawang Biliu
She is a member of Reconstituted Transitional National Legislative Assembly
(TNLA) since 2010. She was elected to parliament on the ticket of SPLM
representing Mayom County , Unity State. She became the Deputy Speaker of
TNLA in 2011 - 2012 after the independence of South Sudan. Hon. Fatima
Nyawang was former Minister of Health in Unity State in 2005 after CPA.

Amb. Hanna Dijok

"Katiba Bannat " or Girls battalions

Chapter 6:
THE POWER OF FEMALE PROTESTERS IN THE FACE OF ABUSE AND GUNS

"You have what it takes to be a victorious, independent, fearless woman,"— Tyra Banks

Protesting is a universal language. When people come together en masse to demonstrate their cause, no matter where they are in the world, it is a powerful expression of strength, unity, and a desire for change. Many women have played important roles in organizing and taking part in protests worldwide. The fight for women's suffrage in the United States began with the women's rights movement in the mid-nineteenth century. Their efforts to lead the movement and protests are often overshadowed by men, who still get more attention and credit for its successes in popular historical narratives and commemorations. In this chapter, we take a look at a few examples from the long tradition of women's protests and marches, from the small to the large, to the worldwide—but each is as important as the next in the fight for human rights, fairness, and equality.

Sudanese women in the revolution against the Bashir regime

The Sudanese revolution that overthrew the rule of Al-Bashir, who ruled Sudan for thirty years, had a special glow. The Sudanese women played an important role alongside men in the peaceful demonstrations. When the revolution erupted on December 19, 2018, women led the protest procession and chanted for freedom, justice, and peace in the loudest voices; the voices that the autocratic government sought to silence. These brave women were not deterred. They stayed put and sang dozens of patriotic and revolutionary songs. These songs ignited enthusiasm and energized the souls. They held banners and slogans which called for the fall of the oppressive regime. They led the way in occupying the streets in the face of arrest, sexual assault, teargas, live bullets, and harassment by security agents calling them prostitutes and worse. Those who were arrested endured various forms of physical and psychological torture, hair cutting, and physical abuse. Security forces killed and raped peaceful protesters. But the courageous Sudanese women were not deterred. Women from a diversity of classes, generations, religions, educational levels, and ethnicities continued to protest. Many did so even though their parents and husbands forbade it.

The active participation of Sudanese women in the revolution was a major turning point in the history of Sudanese women. After the "Muslim Brotherhood" group and its loyalists took

control of and mismanaged the economy, leading to a deterioration of the living conditions of the Sudanese people, women were the biggest casualties. In 1996, al-Bashir passed the Public Order laws that prohibited women from violating certain dress codes and standards of behavior. For example, women could be whipped for choosing to wear pants or not covering their hair, and they were not allowed to spend time with any non-relative man. Additionally, Sudan has one of the highest rates of female genital mutilation (FGM) in the world. The Islamist regime of Bashir also codified the most conservative family law in the region where, among other things, the minimum age of marriage was set at 10 years, and it stipulated that women needed the permission of male guardians to work outside of the marital home. Many protesters saw these regulations as oppressive and contrary to the dignity of women. For thirty years under the Bashir regime, women in Sudan struggled to obtain their basic rights. The 2019 revolution marked the beginning of the end of unjust laws. It gave the Sudanese women a glimmer of hope to reclaim the rights of which they were deprived. Their message in the protest staged at the doorstep of the Ministry of Justice was candid and clear: Justice, peace, equality, and dignity for all.

The atrocities they encountered from the security forces emboldened more women who found more reasons to join the peaceful protests. They organized sit-ins in front of the General Command from April 6, 2019, until the day of the massacre on June 3, 2019. The demonstrations that appeared on social networking sites such as Facebook came in to support the revolutionary movement. Some used these forums

to mobilize for support and to unmask the identity of secret informants for the security apparatus.

Women were not only present in the streets. Their presence and imprints were felt in the professional committees that were established as unions parallel to the unions of authority in government institutions and facilities and contributed to the success of all revolutionary activities, such as organizing demonstrations, civil disobedience, and others. They were actively present in committees of doctors, teachers, lawyers, journalists, and engineers. Housewives also contributed to fueling the flame of the revolution by participating in protest processions, supplying the demonstrators with food and clean water, and providing safe havens for those persecuted by the security services.

The impact of women was also felt beyond the streets and boardrooms. They played significant contributions to women in displacement and refugee camps, and liberated areas, by organizing vigils and demonstrations. The Sudanese women in the diaspora were not left behind. They held vigils in front of Sudan's embassies abroad and several embassies of the free world. They brought the voice of the Sudanese revolution to the world's earshot.

Young Sudanese women from across the divide did not stand back. They were at the forefront, protesting in various ways; in the streets, through art and poetry, and social media. They played a great role in the revolution and became inspiring figures in Sudanese society. One of them was Alaa Salah, a university student, who wore a white Sudanese dress; a dress

that expresses the identity of Sudanese women and was worn by students and female employees as a uniform. Salah composed a revolutionary chant expressing the Sudanese woman (Kandaka) from inside the sit-in square. It was filmed and spread to all parts of the world. Indeed, Salah stole the show and was dubbed as an icon of the 2019 revolution in Sudan

Sudanese women emerged from the revolution as brave women who entered the battlefield where people were threatened with death and sniped with bullets. But this war is far from over. Despite women's participation in the protests before the power-sharing agreement, there is also still much progress to be made in ensuring women's representation in the new government. During the negotiations leading up to the power-sharing agreement, men excluded women from critical meetings. And just like in the case of the Public Order laws and FGM, both women and men must commit to challenging the culture of male domination to increase female representation in government. Building upon the momentum of the Women's Revolution is critical. Increasing female participation in government would aid the further promotion of women's rights as well as send a continuing signal that women can be part of Sudan's new generation of leaders. There are significant cultural and legal barriers to overcome, but Sudanese women have shown they are ready for a fight.

The defiant and brave Ukrainian women who stood up against the Russian invasion

An all-out invasion by Russia on February 24, 2022 turned the battle into an existential fight for Ukraine's very survival as an independent state. Ukrainian women are at the forefront of the humanitarian response and advocating for the restoration of collective human rights and fundamental freedoms.

While the battle against Russia carries on and the men of Ukraine are ordered to fight, the women of Ukraine are stepping up too. In the first days, a lot of young women came wanting to get their hands on a rifle so that they could go out and fight. A few older women in civilian clothes jotted down the personal details of new volunteers into their laptops. Their heroic spirits were stirring.

Olena Zelenska, the first lady of Ukraine, emerged as a symbol of resilience and defiance. She posted an open letter addressed to the world's media, detailing what she described as the "mass murder of Ukrainian civilians." Zelenska repeatedly used social media to highlight the plight of her nation, yet none have been quite as direct as her post which ended with the rallying cry: "We will win. Because of our unity. Unity towards love for Ukraine. Glory to Ukraine!" As her husband, President Volodymyr Zelensky, emerged as the face of Ukrainian defiance of the Russian invasion, Zelenska became increasingly vociferous online to support him and bolster international awareness of their country's plight. When Russia first invaded Ukraine on February 24, Zelensky declared in a video statement that he believed "enemy sabotage groups" had entered Kyiv and that he was their number one target. His

family, he said, was the second target. The whereabouts of his wife and two children remained secret, for security reasons. Nonetheless, Zelenska played an active role on social media, inspiring her people and backing resistance to Russian forces, while garnering support from the rest of the world. On Instagram alone, she garnered 2.4 million followers. The 44-year-old published the open letter on her various social media platforms, as well as on the President's official website, in response to what she said was the "overwhelming number of media outlets from around the world" that had requested an interview with her. She began the impassioned missive -- headlined "I testify" -- by recalling the events of February 24. "Tanks crossed the Ukrainian border, planes entered our airspace, missile launchers surrounded our cities," she wrote. "Despite assurances from Kremlin-backed propaganda outlets, who called this a 'special operation' -- it is, in fact, the mass murder of Ukrainian civilians." Zelenska highlighted the "terrifying and devastating" child casualties, while also describing the horror of babies born in bomb shelters and roads "flooded" with refugees.

Hours after publishing her open letter, Zelenska, who in 2020 was admitted to hospital with Covid-19, updated her Instagram feed with a picture of young cancer patients heading to safety and treatment in Poland. She wrote: "These are young cancer patients from Ukraine. Just yesterday, they were hiding from the shelling in the basements of clinics. Now they are crossing the Polish border on the way to find safety and, most importantly, to continue their treatments. No aggressor in the world can prevent them from winning the battle against the disease!"

In her open letter she reiterated her husband's demand for a no-fly zone, adding: "Ukraine is stopping the force that may aggressively enter your cities tomorrow under the pretext of saving civilians. If we don't stop Putin, who threatens to start a nuclear war, there will be no safe place in the world for any of us." Her message to Russia and the US was loud and clear: STOP WAR. She bravely told the world that a friendly pat on the shoulder was not enough. Sympathy and concern were not sufficient. The world needed to do more by closing the sky or equipping Ukraine with aircraft to enable them to defend their skies by themselves.

Zalenka was not alone. Oleksandra Wysoczanska who lives in Lviv, Ukraine and works at a military hospital is another example of brave Ukrainian women who stood up to be counted during the Russian invasion. Her niece Sabina Malinowska is translating from Poland. "She saw lots of young men with lots of injuries and it's hard to even say how bad it was," said Malinowska. When her aunt isn't at the hospital, she is one of countless women helping where it is needed. And as war rages on supplies are running low; Malinowska is doing what she can from Poland, tapping her network as a member of the Scouts organization. "Somehow all of the network from Scouts worked out in a shocking way. We just all started connecting to each other," she said.

As night falls and Russian forces continue to press through major Ukrainian centers, civilians are arming themselves to protect their cities. Some of the work included setting up pick-up and drop-off locations on both sides of the border to move in donated medical supplies, food, water and more. Her fellow

Scout, Joanna Kula is helping lead the way. She's from Lviv, but is on the move. "We do work with lots of big companies, and our friends and suppliers, and we coordinate the list of needed products," said Malinowska, translating for Kula. "It's really, really lots of voluntary work happening over there," said Malinowska. "It's winter here, so it's not easy. It's really, really brave work." And they are doing the brave work without hesitation. "It's not like someone asked us to do this or like it's willing for us to do this, it's just the moment - someone comes to our country and takes away the place we live," said Malinowska, noting the women of Ukraine will continue to fight for their country. "Men are fighting, they are on the first front, but they need someone on their back front, and this is the ladies' role - this is where we come from."

Liberian women who stopped Liberia's Civil War

In Liberia, women stamped their authorities as crucial contributors to their societies. And as the ones who dare cross ethnic and religious borders to bring lasting peace to their nation. This was evident during the Liberia civil war.

One of the women who played a remarkable role was Ms. Leymah Gbowee, a Liberian peace activist, social worker, and women's rights advocate. Ms. Gbowee is also a Founder and President of the Gbowee Peace Foundation Africa based in Monrovia. Leymah is known for leading a nonviolent movement that brought together Christian and Muslim women to play a pivotal role in ending Liberia's devastating, fourteen-year civil war in 2003. This victory led to the election of Africa's first female head of state, Liberian President Ellen

Johnson Sirleaf, and a new wave of women emerging worldwide as essential and uniquely effective participants in brokering lasting peace and security.

She worked proactively to restore peace and she became the founding member and Liberia coordinator of Women in Peacebuilding Network. She mobilized women who were her fellow Christians to advocate for peace and she collaborated with the Muslims to build a coalition with the Muslim women giving rise to the interfaith movement known as Women of Liberia Mass Action for Peace.

This is a milestone contribution to the country's peace which leads to stability.

Gbowee joined the women in Peace building Network and she became a leader within the Organization where she organized the women from various ethnic groups and religious backgrounds to protest against the then ongoing Liberian conflict. The Women in Peace building Network (WIPNET) demonstrated against the war by fasting, praying, and picketing at marketplaces and in front of government buildings while dressed in white and present in great numbers daily. This made it difficult for them to be ignored and eventually, Gbowee was granted a meeting with Liberia's president Charles Taylor where she pressed for peace.

In 2006, she co-founded the Women Peace and Security Network Africa in Accra, Ghana, and served as the director which was dedicated to promoting women's participation and leadership in peace and security governance on the continent.

Later on in 2012, Leymah launched a new NGO, the Gbowee Peace Foundation Africa, Monrovia, Liberia which provides education and leadership development opportunities for women, girls, and youths which is a great milestone in nation-building.

Gbowee led a women's movement to a hotel where peace negotiations were taking place and dropped on the floor, preventing the men from leaving until they reached a peace agreement. When they tried to leave, Gbowee threatened to rip off her clothes and remain naked, which is considered a curse in Africa. The two teams finally signed the peace agreement, and Gbowee called off the strike. Her consistency and brevity not only earned her the Nobel Peace Prize award but also several other awards such as the Blue Ribbon for Peace (2007) which was awarded by the Women's Leadership Board of the John F. Kennedy School of Government at Harvard University.

Her contribution also is recognized in reproduction health and family planning as a member of the African Women Leaders Network in Reproduction and Family Planning. Gbowee's success and contributions to peacebuilding in Liberia can also be found in her memoirs, Mighty Be Our Powers: How Sisterhood, Prayer, and Sex Changed a Nation at War.

The defiant and brave Afghanistan women against the Taliban

In Afghanistan, during the Anti-Taliban protests, women took up guns in northern and central Afghanistan, marching in the

streets in their hundreds and sharing pictures of themselves with assault rifles on social media, in a show of defiance as the Taliban made sweeping gains nationwide. One of the biggest demonstrations was in central Ghor province, where hundreds of women turned up in their numbers, waving guns and chanting anti-Taliban slogans. They were not likely to head to the frontlines in large numbers because of both social conservatism and lack of experience. But the public demonstrations, at a time of urgent threat from the militants, were a reminder of how frightened many women are about what Taliban rule could mean for them and their families.

"There were some women who just wanted to inspire security forces, just symbolic, but many more were ready to go to the battlefields," said one of the protestors. "That includes me. I and some other women told the governor around a month ago that we are ready to go and fight."

This came at a time when Taliban were sweeping across rural Afghanistan, taking dozens of districts including in places such as northern Badakhshan province, which 20 years ago was an anti-Taliban stronghold. They have since taken over the leadership of Afghanistan after the US withdrew its forces. But the voices of the women were loud and clear. They are ready to continue fighting against the restrictions on women's education, their freedom of movement, and their clothing. Even women from extremely conservative rural areas aspire to more education, greater freedom of movement, and a greater role in their families. They fear that the Taliban rule will take them in the opposite direction.

Women movements and protests staged elsewhere in the world

In 1949, hundreds of female housekeepers staged a protest against low wages. They marched from London's Temple Gardens all the way to Lincoln's Inn Fields. The women, who were members of the Civil Service Union, were being paid 34c an hour and were protesting Sir Stafford Cripps, the Chancellor of Exchequer, for a raise to 40c. The sign they carried read "Cleanliness is next to Godliness. Women cleaners are next to starvation". They also bought new mops to brandish for the occasion.

On August 9, 1956, a group of South African women began a march to protest against the passed laws, which were a form of internal passport designed to segregate the population—and a dominant feature of the country's apartheid system. Led by Lilian Ngoyi, Helen Joseph, Albertina Sisulu, and Sophia Williams-De Bruyn, 20,000 women from all backgrounds marched to Pretoria's Union Buildings to present the prime minister with a petition. The prime minister was not there to accept it, so it was handed over to his secretary as the women sang "wathint' abafazi, wathint' imbokodo", meaning "you strike a woman, you strike a rock". August 9 is now celebrated as National Women's Day in South Africa, to commemorate their courage and strength.

The 2017 Women's March was an example of a huge-scale international protest: an estimated 7 million people marched peacefully all over the world—even in Antarctica— to advocate human rights, freedom, and equality for all. Largely organized through social media, it became the biggest single-

day protest in the United States, with around 1-1.6% of the population attending. One of the most iconic images of the march was the pink "pussyhat", a project that encouraged crafters all over America to knit and sew over 1 million hats to create a lasting visual statement across the march.

AGIR, the Association of Female Indigenous Warriors from Rondônia, was formed to help combat the low participation of women in decision-making in the Indigenous community of Brazil, which is made up of about 15,000 people across over fifty ethnic groups. Emerging in 2015, the members fight for their voices to be heard, holding meetings and participating in demonstrations. One of the issues that are of biggest concern is the mining of Indigenous lands: mining leads to contamination of the environment that damages resources for food and handicrafts, and also has societal implications with the increase in alcohol, drugs, and prostitution it brings.

In 1981, prominent disability rights activist Lesley Hall and others from the Women With Feminist Disabilities Collective bought tickets to the 1981 Miss Australia Quest beauty pageant, which was a charitable event to raise funds for the Spastics Society (now known as Scope). They smuggled in placards, then stormed the stage to protest the sexist portrayal of women and the way the fundraiser contradicted itself by stigmatizing people with disabilities through promoting specific ideals of beauty. Hall opposed the fact that women with disabilities weren't able to enter the beauty pageant as they were not considered beautiful, and brandished a sign that read "Spastic Society oppresses women."

On March 25, 1911, the Triangle Shirtwaist Factory, a producer of women's blouses in Greenwich Village, New York caught fire. It was the practice of its owners to lock the doorways to the stairways and exits to prevent workers from taking breaks or stealing, and this meant that due to lack of escape routes 146 employees died—123 of them women. Widespread outrage and protest against the poor working conditions led to 100,000 people marching to commemorate the victims. This ultimately resulted in a surge in membership of the International Ladies' Garment Workers' Union, one of the largest labor unions in the US and one of the first to have primarily female membership.

Protest marches against the Vietnam war were a frequent occurrence in London, as well as other major cities around the world, and often these ended violently as activists clashed with the police. One of the more peaceful protests took place on February 19, 1968, when over four hundred women in London began a silent march from outside the American Embassy in Grosvenor Square to Downing Street.

After World War II leaders Franklin Roosevelt, Winston Churchill, and Chiang Kai-shek declared that Korea, which had previously been annexed by Japan in 1910, was to become free and independent. However, the Allies agreed that the Soviet Union, the US, and the Republic of China would have a trusteeship over Korea in the five years leading up to this independence. Brandishing signs, including ones reading "Give Me Liberty or Death" and "Thanks For Liberation We Want Korean Gov't Without Trusteeship", members of the Korean

Women's Democratic Party gathered together in 1946 to demonstrate for immediate independence.

Although women have always been at the forefront of the revolutions and fight for human rights across the world, their marginalization in its aftermath is a clear reminder that women need to stay put to ensure that their rights are center stage in the negotiation of a democratic and peaceful future. Women's revolution continues not only to secure a seat at the table but to break down the patriarchal mentality represented in the government as well as in society.

Inner Power

Alaa Salah addressing protesters during the 2019 Sudan Revolution

Ms. Leymah Gbowee, a Liberian peace activist, social worker, and women's
rights advocate.
Source: Columbia University

Afghanistan women protesting
Source: ABC News

Women cleaners protesting their low wages by marching a third of a mile from
London's Temple Gardens to Lincoln's Inn Fields in 1949
Source: Google Arts and Culture

Chapter 7:

VIOLENCE AGAINST WOMEN IN SITUATIONS OF ARMED CONFLICT AND DISPLACE-MENT

"If we are to fight discrimination and injustice against women we must start from the home for if a woman cannot be safe in her own house then she cannot be expected to feel safe anywhere."-Aysha Taryam

Armed conflicts and ethnic cleansing bring their distinct forms of violence against women with them. These can include random acts of sexual assault by both enemy and "friendly" forces, or mass rape as a deliberate strategy of genocide. In this chapter, I will explore the issue of gender-based violence and rape as a weapon during the war using South Sudan Civil War as a case in point. I will particularly focus on the atrocities committed against women from the Juba massacres of December 15, 2013, until today in some parts of the country. At the onset of the war, women, girls, boys and men were targeted based on gender and their ethnicities. Gang rape and rape with objects were used as spoils of war against certain ethnic groups throughout the war.

155

Women's bodies were cut to remove the fetus and children were burned alive because they belonged to another ethnic group. I want to bring to light the reasons why rape is widely used in wars and its implications for peace in South Sudan. I also intend to give instances of rape against women elsewhere in the world and illustrate its relationship with rape in South Sudan Civil War that has raged the country. The key questions that are intended to be answered in this Chapter, therefore, include: What motivates the soldiers to rape women, girls, and boys? What makes the sexual violence in South Sudan different from similar atrocities in other countries during the war? What will the implications of rapes do for peaceful co-existence among the communities torn apart by war?

Sexual violence occurs frequently in South Sudan, especially during the civil war which started in 2013. At the center of these conflicts are two ethnic groups; the Nuer and the Dinka. According to the UN, more than 24,000 women are at risk of rape and sexual violence. The rape targets women, girls, and boys based on their ethnicity. The victims who resist the advances of the attackers are brutally raped with objects and even gang-raped to death according to Zainab Haw Bangura, the UN Special Representative on Sexual Violence in Conflict. With the increase of gang-rape, sexual slavery, forced marriages, and forced abortion in the country, it is important to find out what motivates the perpetrators.

Rape as a weapon of war

Sexual assault is one of the most terrible crimes on earth and it happens every few minutes. In the context of international law,

the Rome Statute of the International Criminal Courts defines rape as a situation where the victim is deprived of her ability to consent to sex, including providing sex to avoid harm or to obtain necessities. The same Rome Statute recognizes rape and other forms of sexual violence by combatants in the time of armed conflict as war crimes. When rape is widely spread and systematically applied against certain populations, it leads to genocide which is a crime against humanity.

In every civil war, sexual assault is used systematically against women and girls as a weapon of war in many ways to intimidate, humiliate, create fear, extract information, and for ethnic cleansing. Women and girls are targeted purposely to demonstrate to men from the targeted ethnic group that they are not capable of protecting their women hence stand no chance of winning the war. They are sending the message that we raped your women because our ethnic group is superior to yours.

In the genocide that occurred in Rwanda, women were sexually assaulted both by individuals, and gangs, sexual assault with sharp objects such as sticks or barrel of a gun, and held as a sexual slaves or mutilated and killed. The Hutu extremist group raped Tutsi women and murdered them after that. According to Erin K. Baines, the perpetrators conceptualized the women as sexes and not ethicized in Rwanda nationalist discourse. In the context of Rwanda, women and girls who were raped during the genocide ranged from the age of 2 years up to over 50 years. The motivation was to dehumanize the very purity of the nation, the women in that particular culture, and to show the men of Tutsi that they were unable to protect their women.

In the time of war, men rape women with the knowledge that it is not acceptable, but they still do it anyway. This rape is done deliberately to inflict pain on the women as well as to their men. In the second half of the 20th century, cases of rape were documented in more than twenty military and paramilitary conflicts. In the 1990s, rape was used as an instrument of ethnic cleansing in the former Yugoslavia and as a means of genocide in Rwanda. In the former Yugoslavia, women belonging to subjugated ethnic groups were intentionally impregnated through rape by enemy soldiers while in Rwanda's case, women belonging to the Tutsi ethnic group were systematically raped by HIV-infected men recruited and organized by the Hutu-led government. It can be said that women were targeted because they are the back born of a nation and a symbol of nationhood. The invasion of the women can therefore be equated as terrorizing the nation. The invaders use it to show their might and to send a message to the men in the enemy's camps that they are weak and incapable of protecting their nation (women). This message is intended to demoralize the enemy's troops and force them to surrender.

In the late 20th century, in part because of the prevalence of rape in the Balkan and Rwandan conflicts, the international community began to recognize rape as a weapon and strategy of war, and efforts were made to prosecute such acts under existing international law. The primary statute, Article 27 of the Geneva Convention Relative to the Protection of Civilian Persons in Time of War (1949), already included language protecting women "against any attack on their honor, in particular against rape, enforced prostitution, or any form of

indecent assault"; this protection was extended in an additional protocol adopted in 1977.

In 1993 the United Nations (UN) Commission on Human Rights (replaced in 2006 by the UN Human Rights Council) declared systematic rape and military sexual slavery to be crimes against humanity punishable as violations of women's human rights. In 1995 the UN's Fourth World Conference on Women specified that rape by armed groups during wartime is a war crime. The jurisdiction of the international tribunals established to prosecute crimes committed in the conflicts in the former Yugoslavia and Rwanda both included rape, making these tribunals among the first international bodies to prosecute sexual violence as a war crime. In a landmark case in 1998, the Rwandan tribunal ruled that "rape and sexual violence constitute genocide." The International Criminal Court, established in 1998, subsequently was granted jurisdiction over a range of women's issues, including rape and forced pregnancy. In a resolution adopted in 2008, the UN Security Council affirmed that "rape and other forms of sexual violence can constitute war crimes, crimes against humanity or a constitutive act concerning genocide."

Rape in Current South Sudan Context

The tragedies that happened in the world's youngest nation, South Sudan have caused great suffering and destruction. The 2013 genocide has been described as "one of the most horrendous human rights situations in the world". Among these human rights violations are many women being beaten,

raped, and killed; and many others forced to watch their daughters, relatives, and friends being raped.

South Sudan's civil war has led to numerous cases of rape and violence against women but underreported. This is so because of the lack of channels, unfavorable conditions, and the fear of reprisals since some of these atrocities are committed by government-allied forces. "It is horrific", as narrated to Human Right Watch by a woman who saw her sister-in-law being raped. She is one of the women who were raped and witnessed the rape committed by the government forces and their allied proxies of Darfur rebels; the Justice and Equality Movement (JEM). At the start of the conflict on December 15, 2013, government soldiers targeted the Nuer women according to witnesses who had seen them being gang-raped. "Survivors and healthcare workers told me the heartbreaking stories of rape, gang rape, abduction, sexual slavery, and forced marriages," said Zainab Haw Bangura, a UN Special Representative on sexual violence in conflict. She also said that the level of rape she witnessed in South Sudan was the worst in her 30 years of career.

During the South Sudan civil war, most rape cases were being reported daily and the number was increasing significantly even in places where the fighting was not taking place. For example, Wau, the capital of Western Bahr El Ghazal State, registered more than two hundred cases in just a month. Can we say that it is because of war? Significantly the state of lawlessness is witnessed now because of the war. In other words, the war led to anarchy which has led to the rise of rape cases in the regions that did not experience the civil wars.

In Unity State after the government occupied the state from the rebels, women and girls of the Nuer ethnic group were raped. They targeted them because they were Nuer women whose husbands and brothers were rebels. After the rebels took control of Bentiu, the capital of Unity State from the government forces, one commander went on air and said, "Now your women have been raped by the Dinka soldiers and JEM rebels of Darfur and they are now pregnant with Dinka children. So, it is your turn to rape their women and girls too. The commander reiterated that the Dinka are not good people and we should not live with them since they raped our wives and girls".

As fighting continued, between the Dinka and the Nuer, women, and children were not spared. The cycle of revenge killings, extrajudicial killings, and rape became the weapons of war during South Sudan's civil war; a new phenomenon that had never existed in the previous civil wars and the inter-communal fighting between the Nuer and Dinka.

In Central Equatoria State, the UN missions in South Sudan Human Right Development interviewed over one thousand witnesses and victims who witnessed the onset of conflict in the capital of South Sudan, Juba. When the fighting started in the barracks, at first the civilians thought that it was intra-military clashes. But hell broke loose when government-allied forces raided the civilian houses and conducted unlawful searches. The government soldiers, from the Dinka, targeted the Nuer men, women, and children. Their mission was clear: to rape and kill. The rape victims were not only women and young girls, but boys as well. They were forced to have sex with

their close relatives and if they refused they were killed. The government soldiers used the face marks to identify the Nuer men and women. Since the Nuer and the Dinka have similar marks, they used the language to test people and those who failed were killed. The Dinka with the same markings as Nuer were also killed. According to UNMISS reports, Nuer men were rounded up and tied and taken to different locations and killed. In the capital, there were reports of mass killing of women, children, and the elderly who were of the Nuer ethnic group. Those who managed to go to UNMISS camps were the only ones that survived the targeted killings. Roads were also blocked by the government forces to search for those who were getting into the city.

In Jonglei State, fighting broke out and the military divided themselves alongside ethnic lines. Over 200,000 people were displaced and 4,800 went to UN Protection of Civilians Sites (PoC). All those who sought UN protection were the Nuer ethnic group. Targeting on ethnicity also took place in Jonglei capital Bor in which the Nuer killed the Dinka and Dinka killed the Nuer. There were reported cases of rapes. Jonglei State witnessed aerial bombardment with cluster bombs by Uganda Defense Forces that were fighting alongside the government of South Sudan. UNMISS reported the cluster's ammunition, but the international community never condemned the use of these banned clusters. Despite the ethnic clashes, some Nuer spared their Dinka neighbors and vice versa. The civilians were forced to participate in the war by the soldiers from their ethnic group.

Upper Nile State has witnessed the severe fighting between the government forces and the SPLA-in Oppositions. The State capital, Malakal, has changed hands between the government and the rebel forces. It was the scene of gross human rights violations and abuse of the civilian population. In Malakal, as in other states of South Sudan where the conflicts have taken place, there were cases of targeted killings, ill-treatment, and sexual abuse of women and girls according to the UN Human Rights reports.

Targeted killings took place in hospitals and churches too where civilians gathered, and people were killed based on their ethnicities. Even though the UN reports do not specify the exact number of rapes and sexual exploitation, the witnesses who survived reported the severity of it.

South Sudan conflict has recorded horrific sexual abuses in which the soldiers rape women and girls and urinate into the mouth of the victims. The media coverage of rapes and other sexual violence is underwhelming because of government censorship. Many journalists who attempted to report disappeared and some of them were put into prisons. Because of such restrictions of media and lack of accessibility to the warfront by different media houses, the exact number of atrocities could not be quantified. The victims who speak of the abuses are also targeted and silenced.

Rape and other forms of sexual violence are a consistent, systematic feature of the conflict that has been used as a tactic of war to displace populations, to disperse and instill fear within particular ethnic groups. The government should not

just acknowledge the prevalence of rape and other abuse but should also act to prevent the scourge of sexual violence and hold perpetrators to account. Right now, South Sudan is at a stage where it is cost-free to rape, where it is cost-free to rape a child of four years old, or it is cost-free to rape a woman whatever her age. As a result, sexual violence has been fueled and exacerbated by this deep culture of impunity, and hence addressing impunity and reversing this culture of impunity is critical. There is an urgent need for legal assistance, the inclusion of a definition of rape and sexual violence in line with international standards in the South Sudanese legislation, and a strengthening of the rule of law. Ending sexual violence in South Sudan is critical to building lasting peace.

The rape and its implications to South Sudan peace building

The civil war in South Sudan has torn apart communities that have a history of intermarriages, living together side by side in peace and harmony. The conflict broke the social fabric that held together these communities. On account of the killing, you see women from one ethnic group killed because of their ethnicity. In the past women were not killed even if there was war between one ethnic group and another because war is believed to be a realm for men alone. The women and children serve as bridges between communities in conflict. They are the ones who usually take messages and inform other communities that this group will attack you tomorrow. But this dynamic has changed in which women, the elderly, and children were killed mercilessly.

For peace to prevail in South Sudan, the communities that were raped and victimized because of their ethnicities would find it difficult to live and forgive one another. In a culture where acts of revenge and retaliation are practiced daily, more dialogue on reconciliation and forgiveness, and admissions of crimes committed are necessary. In most cultures of the South Sudanese communities, rape is taboo and if a person committed rape, people think he is mad. With the current trends of war, the norms are broken due to anarchy. Since rape is culturally condemned, it has great implications on the prospect of peace in South Sudan.

In some ethnic groups, the rapists were killed because of their heinous acts. So, what does that tell about future interventions? To address rape in the context of bringing peace among communities who were affected by conflict, and it has been used as a tool to dehumanize them, great mobilization is required because it would not be easy to bring people together for discussion. Since rape has been instrumental to target one ethnicity it became a tool of conflict and it will impact peace building in the future.

The trauma, scars, and pain sustained in the process

Sexual violence can have devastating psychological, emotional, and physical effects on survivors. These effects aren't always easy to deal with; but with the right help and support, they can be managed.

Post-traumatic stress disorder, sexually transmitted infections, depression, and pregnancy, are just some of the problems

women face due to sexual violence. Not being able to have their needs met makes it very difficult for these victimized women to better themselves and reach their full life potential. Food safety and medical care are top priorities and it is very difficult or even impossible, to do anything without them.

More than 1300 rape cases were recorded in just one of South Sudan's States over five months during the 2013 civil war. Survivors of these crimes will need extensive psychological help because the effects of what they've been through can be profound. It can cause so many problems for them throughout their life. Survivors would carry these burdens forever if not treated or helped to heal. Sadly, these women have been so violated that these horrendous crimes have broken their souls. But society still expects these victimized souls to remain strong for their children and families and even for Survival. But the nightmares, the pain, the rage, the dissociation, and numbness will continue to be there deep within. Their minds are filled with this constant reminder that death might be a better option.

However, there is still hope. There is hope for a life; a life not affected by war. Hope that future generations will live for many more years without constant reminders of horrendous crimes being inflicted on them. Hope that life won't just be trying to make it through another day, but that life will be something to look forward to, in prosperity and fulfillment. Hope that all the broken hearts and the festering wounds will

A victim of sexual violence during the Rwanda Genocide of 1994
Source: BBC

Ms. Zainab Hawa Bangura and I at the United States Institute of Peace. Ms. Bangura is Special Representative of the United Nations Secretary General on Sexual Violence in Conflict.

A victim of sexual violence during the South Sudan conflicts
Source: Amnesty International

Chapter 8:

THE ROLE OF WOMEN IN BUILDING SUSTAINABLE PEACE AND REBUILDING THE NATION

"Many countries have understood that women's equality is a prerequisite for development." ____*Kofi Annan*

S topping a war or conflict is not the same as putting a permanent end to violence. An end to violence marks the beginning of the daunting task of building sustainable peace. This is a long-term process of encouraging people to talk, repairing relationships, and reforming institutions. Protecting civilians, promoting security, reducing violence, and assisting local authorities to take on these activities to promote long-term stability and development, are some of the peacekeepers' roles from the UN and other agencies. For positive change to last, everyone affected by a destructive conflict must be involved in the process of building peace. In this regard, women are critical to peacekeeping success around the world.

Evidence shows that women's involvement in peace negotiations contributes to the quality and durability of peace agreements, as well as a higher number of provisions aimed at political reform and higher implementation rates. This is a theory that has been tested and verified through the excellent work done by UN women peacekeepers all over the world. I can testify to this fact because I have witnessed first-hand and was inspired by the excellent work done by the UN women peacekeepers in my country, South Sudan. I saw these selfless women peacekeepers serving as role models for women's empowerment in local communities and engaging with communities to prevent conflict, promote human rights, and contribute to lasting peace.

I was particularly inspired by Major Suman Gawani, an Indian Army officer and a peacekeeper. Major Gawani has served with the United Nations Mission in South Sudan (UNMISS). As a military observer, Major Gawani was responsible for collecting information through patrolling the villages and the towns. She was an eye and ear of the peacekeeping mission. She moved from village to village to meet the local communities, understand their issues, and investigate cases that happened on the ground including gender-based violence. Apart from supporting the UNMISS force initiatives, she also trained the South Sudan government forces on CRSV-related aspects. The officer also commanded the UN Peacekeepers Day Parade organized by UNMISS. Due to this outstanding contribution to peacekeeping efforts in the UNMISS, Major Gawani was nominated for the prestigious United Nations Military Gender Advocate of the Year Award on May 29th, 2019. She was the first Indian woman peacekeeper to be awarded the UN Military

Gender Advocate Award. It was a great honor for her and her country.

Although they make up a minority of UN peacekeeping missions around the world, women in peacekeeping play a very critical role in preventing and resolving conflicts. They also make peacekeeping missions more accessible to women in the community, including survivors of sexual or gender-based violence. They also promote and support women's participation in peace processes and act as role models for women in the community. "As a woman peacekeeper, I have better access to the community. I have better access and support for local women and children who are majorly subject to the violence," said Major Himika, one of the UN women peacekeepers. She also added that women peacekeepers provide a greater sense of security to the local population and help to reduce conflict and confrontation.

Peacekeeping missions are one of the contemporary methods that the international community seeks to use to institute sustainable peace after conflict. In this regard, the United Nations' traditional peacekeeping role (understood as acting as an impartial interlocutor or monitor) has broadened considerably. Missions now frequently include a long list of state-building roles, including re-establishing police and military forces and building of political institutions.

Sprouting Feminist theorists and contemporary platitudes have advanced the peacekeeping conversation, over security-seeking behavior shaped by masculine notions of militarized security. Post-conflict situations are conventionally characterized as a

formal cessation of violence between armed combatants, ideally transitioning to a hypothetical situation where the state has a respite monopoly on the use of force. It is this shift that peacekeeping missions seek to facilitate, effectuating a wide range of tasks such as disarming combatants, facilitating peace solutions between state and non-state groups, monitoring elections, and constituting capacity for the realization of rule of law in state institutions like police forces and the military.

However, as feminist International Relations scholars have shown, violence against women often persists in the post-conflict period at rates commensurate to, or even larger than, during the conflict period. This encompasses rape and sexual assault, domestic violence, and forced prostitution, as well as those selling sex to alleviate financial insecurity, "sex working." The predominant approach to keeping peace often obscures these kinds of violence.

Issues like gender equality, domestic violence (and human rights) are considered lenient or soft issues, as opposed to the hard or corporeal issues of military security. This understanding of peace, then, is one in which women's security is not central. This has resultantly obliged women to disproportionately bear the brunt burden and consequence of war.

Militarized Masculinity in Peacekeeping Operations

In terms of structural and indirect violence, women are generally sidelined from positions of power and decision-making in reconstruction efforts. They have limited access to

economic resources. High rates of violence and restrictions on women's access to political, economic, and social resources in post-conflict environments limit their eventful participation in the societal building of peace.

The restraints on women's access to resources, such as basic food, housing, and education, make them more susceptible to gender violence. This begins with women's exclusion from peace negotiations and solutions, which instead focus on elite players who are predominantly male, often militarized.

In peacekeeping missions, women are also under-represented. In 1993, women made up only 1% of deployed personnel. That figure had only risen to 3% for the military and 10% for police personnel by 2014. As gender inequality has become increasingly acknowledged, those involved in peacekeeping have ever since paid more attention to the causes and consequences of women's insecurity in post-conflict settings.

In October 2000, the UN Security Council devoted an entire session to Women, Peace, and Security – adopting Resolution 1325 as a result. This resolution calls for a gender perspective to be "mainstreamed" throughout peace operations and for women to be included in peace agreements and post-conflict decision-making – in addition to the protection of women and girls during the conflict. It also emphasized the integration of gender expertise in peacekeeping.

Resolution 1325 calls on all actors to recognize the "special needs" of women and girls in post-conflict societies, to support local women's peace initiatives, and advocate for the protection of women's human rights in the electoral, judiciary,

and police systems. However, consistent with the construction of a gendered understanding of peace discussed above, limitations to the full execution of Resolution 1325 still stand.

Gender discussions in peacekeeping continue to be under-resourced politically and financially, and the gendered elements of post-conflict reconstruction have never been better in missions. Women still experience high rates of post-conflict violence. They are still excluded from peace processes and still ignored in the peace-building policy. This is demonstrated, for example, in national and international attempts to disarm former combatants after conflict and their reintegration into post-conflict society machinations.

This is a post-conflict policy area that feminist scholars have routinely exposed as being highly gendered and exclusionary of women who are former combatants. This can be attributed to constructed gender identities and biases that minimize the idea that women are agents in conflict or involved in war-making and thus, are confined to the passive role of a victim with limited agency. In other words, they are subjects of war rather than objects of the same.

This means that women are not only excluded from disarmament programs because of socially produced gender norms but also that they are unable to access the material and economic benefits that may flow from such programs – or the political and social strides they could make from being recognized as legitimate veterans in post-conflict societies. This example demonstrates the power invested in gendered identities and biases- the ways policy is misshaped and how gender inequality is perpetuated via such policy.

Finally, international interventions, such as peacekeeping missions, also contribute to the continuation of violence post-conflict and are a means by which gendered identities are produced. There have been numerous reports of women targeted through sexual violence as a tactic of war. The issue gained much attention in 2015 and into 2016 when a United Nations whistleblower exposed reports of the commission of sexual abuse of children in the Central African Republic by French peacekeepers. Besides, the United Nations mission in the face of these reports could hold the key in these out-doings. From a feminist perspective, the impunity that peacekeepers enjoy despite rhetorical commitments to zero tolerance – is a result of gendered security imperatives in which militarized security and organizational or statutory coherence of the institution is prioritized over the welfare of the individual.

Women in Peace and Nation-Building

Women's contributions to peace and nation-building have not been acknowledged from ancient times despite their positive and enormous contributions. However, in the recent past, women's effort has come to the limelight as being instrumental in most nations' aspects of peace and nation-building. Over the last few years, there has been an increased number of women in leadership positions in Africa. Their role has shown that women, if given a chance, can be an important asset not just in peace-building initiatives but also in nation-building in general through their attention to detail style of leadership.

The following is a list of some women who have made a positive contribution to peace and nation-building.

Hon. Angelina Jany Teny

Women have worked actively for peace in Sudan, both throughout the decades of civil war and in the various peace processes that ended the war in 2005. It goes without saying that women are key to achieving sustainable peace and development solutions, whether peacebuilding, peacekeeping, or conflict and crisis response. Strong women's caucuses and organizations in both South Sudan and Sudan continue to work for the people's betterment and for resolving internal conflicts within their countries. Angelina Jany Teny, the former South Sudanese Minister of Defence and Veterans Affairs is among these women who are striding forward to realize a better world for her people and particularly women and girls. Most known for her outstanding contributions as an activist for democracy and human rights and educator, Angelina Teny truly has South Sudanese and her fellow African people in mind – and in her heart – as she builds a legacy that would eventually go on to make her one of Africa's most internationally recognized women.

Having been actively involved in successful peace processes as a Minister and human right activist, she has affirmed the role of women in the prevention and resolution of conflicts,

negotiations, peacekeeping, humanitarian responses and post-conflict reconstruction. She believes that the full, equal, and meaningful participation and involvement of women and young people in all efforts is essential for maintaining and promoting sustainable social cohesion and security. This has led her to advocate for stronger representation of women and youth in conflict prevention and peace support processes at all levels.

She is a proud mother of four, a loving wife to Dr Riek Machar Teny, a women's rights activist, and a Great Britain educated. She has risen high the ranks in the male dominated business of politics and governance where she has proven outstanding performance not only in peacebuilding and conflict resolution but also in the energy sector. While serving as a state minister of Energy and Mining in 2005, she was part of a team that established an autonomous Government of South Sudan (GoSS) and defined a process to move towards a referendum on full independence.

At a November 2006 conference, she headed a team that noted that there had been considerable controversy over the Ministry of Energy and Mining when the Government of National Unity was being formed. The oil industry had been developed during the civil war as a means to finance that war, at great human cost, and military concerns had dictated the structure of the industry. Now the government was struggling to organize the National Petroleum Commission (NPC), but the SPLM had confidence in the process. Through her leadership as the minister in charge, she set Sudan on the path of developing the oil sector in order to support sustainable peace

and promote environmental conservation. She did so by ensuring that those aggrieved during war got redress, and advocated for oil production that is sensitive to social responsibility. She called for review of contracts and compensation of the local people. She also called for environmental issues to be addressed.

Indeed, Hon. Angelina Teny has made tremendous contributions toward building a sustainable peace and human rights in her country. Through her achievements, she is a testament that women participants in peace processes are usually focused less on the spoils of the war and more on reconciliation, economic development, education and transitional justice – all critical elements of a sustained peace. This, therefore, means that the inclusion of women can and must take many forms, especially in the effort to address rising global violent conflict that since the end of the Cold War has occurred within states, with armed insurgencies or civil wars tearing countries apart. The end to these conflicts cannot be forged through only a top down peace process, with only armed actors at the negotiating table. Instead, it requires a more inclusive process—one that includes women playing more pivotal roles in building a peace from the bottom up as well as from the top down, engaging multiple stakeholders. Parties must come together not just in the capital city but also at the local level where communities are confronted with a host of critical issues that left unaddressed could unravel any peace deal.

She has also played a role in mitigating climate change impacts by being among the most vocal, and those leading the charge

in terms of action. In her words, the coming decades bring many challenges, but with equity and inclusion as a guiding principle, we can make the future more sustainable, peaceful and just.

H.E Joyce Banda

Joyce Banda was the Malawian President from April 2012 to May 2014 after the death of President Bingu. She also doubled up as an advocate for women's rights. She became a Minister of Gender and Child Welfare as a member of parliament before she became the president. Her contribution to enacting the Violence Bill which had failed severally was a milestone achievement in her political life.

Joyce has been involved in many grassroots projects since she was 25 years of age. She always had to bring about policy change, particularly in the Malawi system of education. The change was achieved through The Joyce Banda Foundation; whose main role was to Better Education and through the foundation many clinics were established, rural development was achieved in partnership with the Jack Brewer Foundation hence positive contribution to nation-building. She founded the Young Women Leaders Network, the National Association of Business women, and The Hunger Project in Malawi.

In 2010, Joyce Banda became a member of the Global Leaders Council for Reproductive Health, a committee committed to advancing reproductive health for lasting development and prosperity. In 2012, Joyce took a pay cut of 30% on her salary

and announced that the government would sell the presidential jet. This was part of her initiative to curb the difficult economic conditions and reduce public expenditure. Through her, entrepreneurship in the country improved by establishing various enterprises such as Ndekani Garments, Akajuwe Enterprises, National Association of Business Women (NABW), and Kalingidza Bakery. She achieved so much and she won many international awards and honors, hence one of the greatest women in Africa to contribute to the peace and nation-building agenda.

H.E Ellen Johnson Sirleaf

H.E Ellen Sirleaf is the former president of Liberia who has also left a mark in women's leadership and made history in the world. Ellen achieved the mark of peace-making through her role that saw her establishing a Truth and Reconciliation Commission that helped the country heal after the tragic civil war of the 1990s.

Her term in office was characterized by achieving free and compulsory elementary school education and also passed the Freedom of Information Bill on October 4, 2010, which raised Liberia as the first West African country to achieve this kind of law.

Among her great achievements, Johnson also formed the Zero Tolerance Campaign Against Child Abuse and established good relations with mainland China. She also put in place policies that restored optimistic relations donors and the

international community in the country after decades of civil war and dictatorship.

H.E Johnson also secured Liberia's debt reliefs from the United States and Germany and helped the country pay about 60% of its debt obligation to the International Monetary Fund (IMF). Sirleaf prioritized keeping the nation's annual borrowing to 3% of Gross Domestic Product (GDP). This policy stabilized the country's economic position, attracting many foreign direct investments into the Liberian economy. She is also remembered as an advocate of peace and reconciliation in Liberia, which she achieved by inviting opposition members into the cabinet. Her main goal when she was elected to the office was to rebuild the country's economy and infrastructure which had been greatly affected by decades of conflict and instability. She also worked to promote unity and reconciliation within the country.

Johnson Sirleaf also addressed the infamous culture of corruption in Liberia that had been rampant for some time by firing the entire staff of the Ministry of Finance. In her regime as the president, Liberia also saw the lifting of UN sanctions and arms embargoes that had been in place since the Civil Conflict. UN Peacekeeping troops also stopped being in charge of handling security concerns in Liberia during Sirleaf's presidency. Full responsibility for matters such as peace was given back to Liberia's army and police. This promoted peace, security, and stability tremendously in the country.

H.E. Dr. Arikana Chihombori Quao

Dr. Arikana of Zimbabwe is another significant female figure who has had a great impact on peace and nation-building. She is a medical doctor and an activist. Apart from that, she is a speaker, diplomat, educator, founder of medical clinics, and entrepreneur.

Dr. Arikana served as the African Union Ambassador to the United States of America. She is hailed for her commitment to reinforcing the longstanding and historical, cultural, and economic relationship between Africa and the United States of America. She played a major role in reinforcing the African Union's strategic partnerships with the United States based on mutual values and interests. She has also served as the Chair of the African Union-African Diaspora Health Initiative (AU-ADHI), where she mobilized the African Diaspora health professionals to address the healthcare crisis on the continent of Africa hence an immense contribution to the people of Zimbabwe.

She worked tirelessly to undertake, develop and maintain relationships between the African Union and the Executive and Legislative branches of the US Government, the Africans in Diaspora, and the Bretton Woods Institutions. This was aimed at unifying and bringing peace between the African Community and the International Community. She has countless prestigious honors and awards such as the Achievement Award (1996) and the African Women of

Excellence Award (2015) for her great contributions to the cause of Africa at large.

Prof. Wangari Maathai

Prof. Wangari Maathai of Kenya is the epitome of women's contribution to peace and nation-building not only in Kenya but internationally by winning different awards for her commitment to serve the people and having an interest in peace and the environment at heart. She was the first woman in East and Central Africa to become a Doctor in Philosophy and also the first African woman to receive the Nobel Peace Prize. In her country, she was actively involved in Kenya's struggle for democracy and mobilized women for peaceful demonstrations. She founded the Green Belt Movement which was focused on environmental conservation and women's rights. The movement was aimed at countering deforestation to help save the subsistence of the agricultural population. She also contributed to converting the Kenyan Ecological debate into mass action reforestation. Her immense contribution to environmental conservation and sustainable development, democracy, and peace never went unnoticed. A milestone contribution was also to organize and pay a stipend to women which acted as a motivation for women to work harder to achieve the goal of planting many trees in different regions. She is also recognized for her efforts to reduce poverty and push for democracy through her activism journey. The capability to get more funding saw her extend the Green Belt Movement outside the country through Africa which led to the Pan-African Green Belt Network which many other countries came

to learn of various strategies to combat desertification, deforestation, water crisis, and rural hunger.

Apart from being an environmental activist, she pushed to unite the opposition and fair elections in Kenya. When ethnic clashes occurred, she traveled with friends and press to areas of violence to encourage them to cease fighting hence her immense contribution to the peace in Kenya. She was also behind the development of sustainable development, democracy, and peace and she was the first woman to win the prestigious award for her holding of peace congresses.

Wangari Maathai is internationally recognized also for her persistent struggle for democracy, human rights, and environmental conservation. She has numerous awards and prizes from various recognized institutions and individuals.

Awadeya Mahmoud Koko

Sudan has suffered brutal civil wars and political uncertainty for decades. Amidst these challenges, the Sudanese have learnt the art of fighting for their survival. This has made them become resilient and determined in the face of adversity. Among them is Awadeya Mahomoud, a humble Sudanese woman who overcame numerous hurdles to rise to the top. Her journey started as a tea seller in makeshift kiosks along the streets, and today she owns chains of top hotels and restaurants. From a humble beginning, and numerous hurdles, she has now employed 8,000 women and counting.

Inner Power

Born in 1963 in a patriarchal society in South Kordofan, Sudan, the odds were always stacked against her. She grew up in a society where women faced all forms of violence and discrimination. She was a victim, having been denied access to basic education and healthcare by being a woman. She lived amongst many victims, most of whom had resigned to fate.

Like the proverbial old donkey that stepped on the soil thrown at it to emerge out of the hole, she used the challenges she faced as a motivation to bring positive change. She believed that through hard work and advocacy, she would liberate herself and other women as well from the York of poverty, ignorance and abuse. This dream appeared as a mirage since she was an illiterate village girl who was expected to get married and serve her husband and children. Indeed, she got married and as a housewife, society expected her to focus on raising her children and serving her husband. This she did, but she did not shut out her dream. Like an iron that has gone through fire, she had gone through difficult experiences which had hardened her. Nothing would stand between her and her determination to bring a positive change not only to herself and family but also to the community. So, in 1986, she started selling tea to earn a living. She did not stop at that. She started enlightening women to stand up and demand for their basic rights. Education, she believed, was not a preserve of the male. They, too, as women, had the right to access this vital key that would unlock the golden door to freedom, access to proper healthcare and self-reliance. She inspired women to stand up and fight for their basic rights. She mobilized resources to empower women and used workshops and roadshows to enlighten them. Always in the thick of the struggle, she

endured threats and strong opposition from male dominated community leadership. She was sailing against the tides but she was not ready to back off. The ship had left the shore and nothing was going to stop it from sailing. She remained steadfast in her mission.

Her resilience paid. The business she started from scratch was thriving as demand for her sweet tea grew. She attracted customers from all walks of life who thronged her makeshift kiosk to have a taste of her tea. Her name and cause became known far and wide. She did not only receive tea customers but also several women who sought her advice and help. Her advocacy and business were paying off. She used her profits to assist the needy, especially women and children.

In 1990, in collaboration with the rural women, Awadeya founded a social enterprise organization dubbed Women's Food and Tea Sellers' Cooperative and the Women's Multi-Purpose Cooperative which offered pro bono legal services to its members. The major objective of the Organization was to offer free legal services, education and healthcare to women in rural areas. The organization quickly gained traction and soon expanded to other nearby villages, impacting the lives of thousands of women. Despite her success, Awadeya never forgot her roots and remained humble and grateful for all that she had accomplished.

Her life took an unanticipated turn when she got arrested for failing to service her loan. Since most of her profits were going to the support of the community, she had to borrow at some point to keep her business afloat. This turn of event was

devastating not only to her but also her family and the community members who depended on her. She endured 4 years in prison struggling to survive and give hope to her family and the women who looked up to her. She had to keep the fire burning despite the huge setback, and hope was her only tool of trade.

While in jail, she did not give in to fate. She turned her time there to a moment of reflection and strategizing. She knew that she had a life after jail and that she had to continue the work she had started. Her family needed her and so were the women. So, after the four long years in prison, she got out of jail feeling rejuvenated and more determined. She was stronger than ever. With great zeal and fresh determination, she returned to her community. The spirit within her and love for her people was at its best. She was like a healed broken bone. She revived an 8,000 members Cooperative Khartoum which she had founded before. She approached with fresh determination and a new sense of purpose. The growth was steady, so after several years, this organization thrived and became a beacon of hope for women in the rural areas across the country. This did not come on a silver platter. She faced numerous challenges but she did not stagger nor give in. Her mission of uplifting women economically and liberating them from oppression was unstoppable.

Her effort did not go unnoticed. Several regional and international human rights organizations, both non-government and government sponsored, recognized her great work. She was invited to speak at national conferences on women's rights. Her story of courage and determination

inspired many others to take up the cause and join her in her fight for equality and justice for women in rural areas.

On the 28th day of March 2016, the United States' Department of State Honors announced her as one of fourteen recipients of the International Women of Courage Award. The Award is also referred to as the U.S. Secretary of State's International Women of Courage Award. It is an American award presented annually by the US' government to women around the world who have shown leadership, courage, resourcefulness, and willingness to sacrifice for others, especially in promoting Women's rights.

Awadeya Mahmoud's story is a testament to the human spirit and the resilience of the people of Sudan. Despite the hardships she faced, she never lost sight of her goals and persevered through adversity. Her unwavering spirit and commitment to her family serve as an inspiration to us all and remind us of the importance of perseverance in the face of adversity. Awadeya's story inspired many people and showed them that with hard work, determination, and a little bit of luck, anything is possible. She proved that no matter where you come from or what challenges you face, you can still achieve your dreams if you don't give up. And so, Awadeya lived a long and happy life, surrounded by love, success, and respect of her community, a true inspiration to all who knew her.

Hon. Jemma Nunu Kumba

It is not about men against women, but there is evidence to show through research that when you have more women in public decision-making, you get policies that benefit women,

children and families in general. So, women tend, when they're in parliament, for example, to promote women's rights legislation. When women are in sufficient numbers in parliaments they also promote children's rights and they tend to speak up more for the interests of communities, local communities, because of their close involvement in community life. One such woman who has left a mark in the political and governance scene is Hon. Jemma Nunu Kumba, the former Minister of Gender, Child and Social Welfare of South Sudan. Having founded the Sudan women Parliamentary Caucus in 2004 at the start of the comprehensive peace agreement, Hon. Nunu Kumba has always had the interest of her community at heart.

In the 1990s, Kumba worked as administrator of a company with ties to the Sudan People's Liberation Army (SPLA) and then as a coordinator for the New Sudan Council of Churches. Hon. Kumba has been deeply committed to peace building and post-conflict reconstruction. In 2002, she participated in peace talks on behalf of SPLM in Kenya. After the Comprehensive Peace Agreement (CPA) in 2005, she served as a member of parliament in Khartoum. Kumba is a member of the SPLM party. She has proven, through her involvement in peace processes, that women have a unique and powerful perspective to bring to the negotiating table. She brought to the limelight how women suffer disproportionately during armed conflict and often advocated most strongly for stabilization, reconstruction and the prevention of further conflict. Moreover, her engagement in the transitional processes and post-conflict governments helped increase the legitimacy of nascent institutions, decreased government corruption,

broadened the political agenda, promoted consultative policymaking and encouraged collaboration across ideological lines and social sectors.

Hon. Kumba is also a champion for education. When her husband was appointed Sudan People's Liberation Movement (SPLM) representative to Namibia, Kumba moved with him. While in Namibia she enrolled at the University of Namibia, studying Economics and Management Science, and graduated with Bachelors Degree in Public Administration and Political science from 1999 to 2002. She has proven that Higher Education is one of the most important means of empowering women with knowledge, skills and self-confidence. It brings a reduction in inequalities and helps in improving their status within the family. She believes that higher educational achievements of women can have ripple effects within the family and across generations.

Honourable Kumba's active participation in politics is also an inspiration to women. She was the first woman to serve as governor after the CPA. She was appointed Governor of the Western Equatorial State in 2008. She lost the April 2010 election but this did not kill her spirit. In June 2010, she was appointed as GOSS Minister of Housing and Physical Planning. On 26 August 2011 Hon. Jemma Nunu was reappointed the Minister for Housing and Physical Planning in the Cabinet of South Sudan. On January 9 2012, Hon. Jemmac was appointed as a member of the National Constitution Review Commission (NCRC). On 3rd August 2013, President of South Sudan Salva Kiir Mayardit shuffled several ministers and deputies, moving Kumba to the Ministry of Electricity,

Dams, Irrigation & Water Resources. By July 2016, she was Minister of Wildlife Conservation and Tourism.

In October 2015, President Kiir Mayardit, appointed Hon. Kumba to serve as Deputy Secretary General of SPLM. At the same time, Salva Kiir dissolved national secretariats and tasked Hon. Kumba recommended new party secretariats. She replaced Anne Itto Leonardo in the position of deputy secretary general of SPLM. Kumba was sworn in on 13 November 2015. Hon. Kumba was appointed Minister of Gender, Child and Social Welfare in 2018. After the signing of the R-ARCSS, in 2019, she was appointed as the Minister of Parliamentary Affairs. On 23 July 2021, Hon. Jemma was nominated by the SPLM Leaderships as SPLM Candidate for the position of Speaker of the Revitalized Transitional National Legislative Assembly.

Through her rise and rise in politics and ministerial positions, Hon. Kumba is a living testimony that women's participation in politics helps advance gender equality and affects both the range of policy issues that get considered and the types of solutions that are proposed. She has proven that whether a legislator is male or female has a distinct impact on their policy priorities, making it critical that women are present in politics to represent the concerns of women and other marginalized voters and help improve the responsiveness of policy making and governance. She is an evidence that as more women are elected to office, there is also a corollary increase in policy making that emphasizes quality of life and reflects the priorities of families, women, and ethnic and racial minorities. Women's political participation has profound positive and democratic

impacts on communities, legislatures, political parties, and citizen's lives, and helps democracy deliver.

These female leaders have made a significant impact in peace and nation-building, they have made extraordinary progress and resisted the political barriers and proved the contrary, women's position in leadership and nation-building can no longer be overlooked. They play equal roles and can be great assets to various initiatives on the grassroots level and the overall building of the nation. They are an important component in achieving an equitable, peaceful, and more prosperous society.

While the journey of women in leadership and the role they play in nation-building has been long and bumpy, their determination and commitment have yielded fruits.

Women are important agents for creating stability in the lives of their families and promoting reconciliation and peace even under very difficult and traumatic situations. However, women's peace-building potential has had no significant impact on policies and decisions relating to conflicts because of their absence from the decision-making processes and bodies in the region. It is important to give attention to the situation for women and their concern over peace and development and to strengthen their role in the promotion of peace and development not only in Africa but also in the world at large.

Major Suman Gawani
She was the First Indian selected for the prestigious United Nations Military
Gender Advocate Award in 2019.
Source: United Nations, Geneva

Angelina Jany Teny
The Champion for Peace and Sustainable Development

Joyce Banda was the Malawian President from April 2012 to May 2014 after the death of President Bingu.

Ellen Johnson Sirleaf is a Liberian politician who served as the 24th President of Liberia from 2006 to 2018.
Source: West Africa Brief

My good friend H.E. Dr. Arikana Chihombori Quao, she's a significant female figure who has had a great impact on peace and nation-building.
Source: by Peter Gatkouth Wadar at African Union office in Washington DC

Wangarĩ Muta was a Kenyan social, environmental and political activist and the first African woman to win the Nobel Peace Prize

Mrs. Awadeya Mahmoud
and I at the United States Institute of Peace.

The former U.S. Secretary of State John Kerry presented the International Women of Courage Award to Mrs. Awadeya Mahmoud Koko.

Hon. Jemma Nunu Kumba, the leader who brought positive change

Chapter 9:
WOMEN'S LIVES AND EXPERIENCES POST-WARS

"Don't ever make decisions based on fear. Make decisions based on hope and possibility. Make decisions based on what should happen, not what shouldn't," – Michelle Obama

During the Second World War, women proved that they could do "men's" work, and do it well. With men away to serve in the military and demands for war material increasing, manufacturing jobs opened up to women and upped their earning power. Post-war periods are crucial in shaping future developments. They are generally times of hope for a brighter future because they carry endless opportunities for massive transformation. On the other hand, they also bring about profound social, political and economic instabilities. These transition periods affect women and men differently and have a strong impact on women's lives and identities. For example, periods following the end of WWI and WWII are considered as turning points for women's rights and roles in society. In this chapter, I will share personal experiences of women who overcame atrocities committed

against them during war and how they built their lives, contributing to their nations' economies.

South Sudanese women building their lives and nation

Women across South Sudan suffered immense harm as the result of the civil war. Many lost their lives, their families, their homes, and their jobs. After the signing of the peace deal, they are playing a significant role in the recovery and rebuilding effort.

In the village of Chahari in Eastern Equatoria state, the state once considered a safe and fertile area of South Sudan, lives Nadia, a single parent whose husband disappeared during war. Her children and his two older brothers depend solely on her. Nadia is hoping to find a relatively peaceful life in this remote, rural area, far from the fighting engulfing the cities and larger towns.

Still, providing her children with enough food to eat is a struggle. A famine fueled by drought and fighting has ravaged the region for four years. With husbands absent, women live by their wits, farming, caregiving, and working on side businesses to generate more income. Away from the frontline of the conflict, they are the ones upholding the country.

"The role of a man here is only to look after cattle and go for cattle raiding," Olia says. "Most of the agriculture and caregiving activities are for women." Livestock is very important for local ethnic groups, as it works as a sort of currency.

Women in South Sudan are also working as caregivers to support fellow women affected by war to access health care. They pack the equipment, drugs and mats onto their bicycles and move from one village to another. "We are carrying out this service to the people who are not reachable by normal facilities," said Olia, one of the volunteers. Pushing hard on the pedals, the women travel to four different villages each week, visiting pregnant women and looking for malnourished children. Their team represents the only healthcare that most locals will see in their lifetime.

Olia struggles to make ends meet, as she cares for her six children by herself. "My partner died in war," she explains. At night, after attending visits and workshops, she sells home-brewed alcohol to make some extra money.

Five years ago, Mary Nyakang watched her husband die. "They came into our house and killed him in front of me and the children," the 39-year-old mother of five said. "They" were South Sudan government soldiers. Nyakang, who lives in Akobo, said it took years to rebuild her life and provide for her children.

After war broke out between the government troops of South Sudan's president, Salva Kiir, and forces loyal to the former vice president, Riek Machar, Nyakang escaped with her children from the capital, Juba, walking for six days in the bush before reaching Akobo.

"I was worried when I lost my husband, because I had nothing," Nyakang said. "But if I stayed idle, my children would have died."

When a woman's husband dies in South Sudan, any property owned goes back to the man's family. It's up to them to decide if they want to support his widow and the children. Nyakang's in-laws didn't give her anything after he died, she said.

So for years in Akobo, Nyakang risked her life collecting firewood in the forest, where women are often raped or abducted by armed men or rival tribes, to sell at market. But after two years of barely scraping by, in 2016 Nyakang was given the opportunity to run the town's first women's hair salon. She was supported by Oxfa, an organization that supports the salon, helping improve the lives of widows by providing them with hair-braiding skills and business training.

Braids hang from the tin walls of the salon, while eager clients sit on the floor admiring their new looks in the mirror. Adjacent to the women's rooms is a tiny barbershop with two seats for men.

While it began as a small startup, the salon grew and employed fifteen women and seven men, serving ten customers each day and bringing in more than $100 a week in total. In a good month, Nyakang takes home 4,000 South Sudanese pounds ($30), more than ten times what she was making collecting firewood.

"What I like about this program is that it is community-based," Nicolo' Di Marzo, deputy country director for Oxfam, said. "We always talk about women's empowerment, but what does that mean in concrete terms?"

For Di Marzo, the answer to that is independence. He said the success of the program is that it enables women to identify solutions for themselves, while increasing their confidence and giving them a voice within their communities. Since the opportunity at the salon was provided for her, Nyakang was able to take charge of deciding what the business needs to grow, what services to offer, and which prices to set.

Nyakang was able to be included in community discussions due to her business. Before starting in the salon, she didn't even have a seat at the table in community meetings. The project also acted as a safe space for women, many of whom have been abused and feel lonely.

When Marsa Wanyag's husband was killed during intra-tribal clashes, his parents gave her a single cow, and allowed her and the three children to lodge at their house. But when fighting broke out in their town near Akobo in 2015, Wanyag's in-laws had to take in their other son's family, and threw the widow and her young children out onto the street.

"They wouldn't support me anymore; they just said, 'Go and survive'," Wanyag said. Like Nyakang, Wanyag walked to Akobo, where she started doing odd jobs to make ends meet. After a year, she began making and selling bread at a bakery, together with twenty other women. Through the bread-making program, Wanyag brought in 2,000 South Sudanese pounds a week (around $15), which allowed her to buy food and soap for her children.

Although she said working at the bakery has lifted a huge burden, she still worries about the children's future. In her

culture, one man's children can never be supported by another – even if the woman remarries. Wanyag said it will be up to her to send her children to school and provide for them for the foreseeable future.

"The biggest challenge is this responsibility of having to do the work of a woman and a man," she said.

Although both the salon and the bakery have been vital for the survival of women in Akobo, the country's current economic crisis compounds the inherent challenges of being a single parent. Both Wanyag and Nyakang are able to put food on the table, but they still struggle with school fees and uniforms for their children.

Women who can't afford to send all their children to school often hold their daughters back to help with the housework. Nyakang's three girls go to school only part-time, she said, as she needed them around the house and can't afford the fees.

Pasca Kole, a 42-year-old refugee woman from South Sudan living in the Pagirinya Settlement in northern Uganda. In July 2016, when the war reached her village in Pagere county, South Sudan, Kole escaped, along with her three children aged 14, 7 and 3 years. She was eight months pregnant at the time, expecting her fourth child. It was not an easy journey.

Heavily pregnant, traumatized and now responsible for all her children, as her husband had stayed behind, Kole's life as a refugee in Uganda was fraught with challenges.

"I came bare handed," she explained. "I got a plot of land, but I couldn't construct a house by myself because I was sick. I could not send my children to school. Imagine someone who used to work in an office, now depending on handouts."

Kole is among the estimated 1,061,000 refugees from South Sudan who have crossed over the border since 2013. Most of them don't know if and when they would go back to their home country. In these situations of protracted crises, needs are complex and long-term. Beyond food and shelter, women and girls also need psychosocial therapy to overcome the severe trauma they have experienced.

Funded by the United Nations Central Emergency Response Fund and the Embassy of Norway, UN Women and its implementing partner Transcultural Psychosocial Organization (TPO) is providing cognitive behavioral therapy to 5,233 women since 2016. Kole enrolled into group therapy with twelve other women suffering from trauma and post-traumatic stress. The programme also offers entrepreneurship and leadership training to women so that they can start living productive lives.

The therapy group became a lifeline for Kole. The members met every two weeks to share their stories and problems and produced solutions. For example, Kole's group supported her to build a house and helped her enroll her children in school. Kole gave birth to a baby girl and now her husband has also joined her in Uganda.

"I used to have a lot of worries because of what I went through. But when members of the group started sharing their

stories, I cried throughout the session," shared Kole. "Their stories were horrible. I realized I was not alone. In fact, my problems were smaller compared to some of theirs. That's how I finally started coping with my situation. The group gave me hope and courage to live again."

Immaculate Anyango, a social worker who works with the groups explained that Kole's group has completed the biweekly therapy sessions and now meets twice a month, as a support network. "We empowered them, and now they continue to meet on their own to discuss how to improve their lives."

Saluwa Grace, 25, further elaborated: "As group members, we love each other. We are united and work together. For example, the food ration we get is not enough, but no member has to sleep on an empty stomach. Fellow members share their food. If it is about buying medicine or books for children, we collect some money from each member and contribute."

The groups also help in diffusing tension between family members and reduce the risk of domestic violence. "Whenever I have domestic problems, I share with my group," said Grace. "One day, my husband beat me up and burnt all my clothes. I talked to my group members for advice. They visited my home and counselled both of us about the benefits of ending violence in our home." Grace and her husband are living peacefully now, and have also learned anger management skills.

"Today our faces are shining. There is a lot of change in our lives," added Kole, stressing on the need for continued

support. "What we went through cannot disappear at once, it's a process."

To build women's resilience further, the programme has provided start-up funds to the groups to raise goats, make and sell bedsheets and other handcrafts, and invest in small savings schemes. It also provides legal aid and organizes community dialogues to prevent domestic violence and child marriage.

"Now that women have overcome trauma, and are earning some income, they feel they have more voice. Many of them have started sending their children to school and meeting their basic family needs," said UN Women acting Deputy Country Representative Anna Mutavati, adding, "We are now scaling up the program with new funding from the Government of Norway, to increase the opportunities for women to lead and participate in refugee and host population decision-making processes, enhance adult education and vocational skills, as well as improve their economic opportunities."

As for Kole, she is raising goats and saving money now. Her group received 500,000 Ugandan shillings (USD 130) from the programme and bought six goats. "Our goats reproduced and the number has already doubled," she said with a big smile. She is also the chairperson of the therapy groups and mobilizes the members to meet regularly.

South Sudanese women are also playing active roles in policy making by fighting for their rightful place in the decision-making table. Years after the signing of the peace deal and civil wars, they are playing a significant role in the recovery and rebuilding effort. The revitalized peace agreement requires 35

percent representation of women in all governance institutions. The country has appointed its first female Speaker and a number of women Parliamentarians, but it is still far from meeting the target set. In response, the United Nations Mission in South Sudan is supporting efforts to increase the participation of women in leadership roles. Working in partnership with the South Sudan Women's Empowerment Network and generous donors, the Mission hold workshops for young women members of the reconstituted Transitional National Legislative Assembly to build their capacity.

Dr. Pricilla Nyangyang Makuac, who has served as South Sudan's deputy minister of Gender, Child, and Social Welfare, and a member of the Women Waging Peace Network (part of the Institute for Inclusive Security), framed the importance of the women's contributions to building their nation: "Its women who fought for independence. It's our country. We made it. Now, when it's time for South Sudan to tell the world, 'Here we are'…women need to be there. In this development plan, we should be able to see ourselves'.

Women in South Sudan have actively participated in decision-making, in which they prioritized four steps that, if taken, would put the rest of the development plan on a fast track:

• **Banking**: Start-up funding of a minimum of $10 million for a "Women's Bank." Since most banks require collateral and most women don't own property, it's essential to have a bank that provides low-interest loans to women, accepting social collateral (where women as a group guarantee that if one defaults the others will pay). Initiating that funding would bring

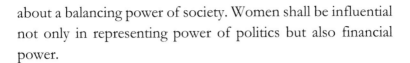

about a balancing power of society. Women shall be influential not only in representing power of politics but also financial power.

That's to realize that power is not just politics but influence that goes along with several factors including financial power. Power as an influence makes people influential rather than forceful. For example financial influence is institutionalized through establishment rather than rationalized through good theory. To realize that in society the first action to be taken is to design policies that advocate for that. By giving that chance to women that shall make it easier for a state to progress more rapidly. I must argue that it requires the change of mentality from a society to take such actions simultaneously to override current patriarchal reality. So materialized new ways of thinking in men as well can be far greater than if that mentality is nurtured in women alone. We need a continued education and upbringing to consolidate that new establishment to enable the society to take that route.

• **Agricultural support**: agriculture is another powerful tool of development. As the banking sector is, agriculture is a powerful tool of progress as they always said. If you need to know a civilized society, look at how they treat women. A state must ensure that 25 percent of agricultural investment is targeted toward women farmers. In South Sudan, 85 percent of the population works in or depends on agriculture—and the vast majority of farmers are women. To grow the economy, women need access to credit for modern equipment and training to know how to use it. They also need a voice in land rights and decisions to build feeder roads that make it possible to get their

goods to market. The policy of prioritizing women could be easy because the majority of farmers are women. You are not going to create a women's society of farmers from the crash. They are already there in the sector.

• **Literacy**: for suggestions above to improve such as Bank and agriculture, increasing education and literacy is required. Doubling the number of adult women who are literate is paramount. Right now, only a staggering 12 percent of adult women can read and write. In some states it's as low as 3 percent. It takes six months to make a woman functionally literate. There must be a policy of a state to assist women to learn.

• **Oil revenues**: Making certain that half the community development funds that come from oil revenue are allocated to women's health, education, economic well- being, and physical security. Now that South Sudan has full control over its vast resources, women want to be sure all citizens share in the wealth and avoid the dependency inherent in the "resource curse. Balance of power in the society is needed. How to create balance between patriarchal influence and matriarchal? The answer is how the Country has laid its policies on resources distribution and ownership of properties. There must be policies to manage and guide the behavior of tyrants and monsters of society.

The case of Central Africa Republic

By creating vibrant economic networks, women in the Central African Republic are coming to terms with the violence they have suffered during their country's civil war.

The bakers of Bamingui have lost loved ones to war. Rebel soldiers drive past their roadside bread ovens daily. A specter of violence remains. Regardless, Yvette Abaka and her female baking collective make dough and roll with it.

In this impoverished, rebel-held corner of the Central African Republic (CAR), this group of mothers came together to better their lot. Since then, their loaves have become a hit in the wider community, promoting the women as their families' breadwinners and promising further, quietly profound, change.

"This bakery makes us more powerful than before," said Abaka, the group's leader and a 50-year-old mother of two. "My husband respects my work. Now I am his equal."

In this turbulent country, scarred by years of conflict, Abaka's bakers are not the only people hoping for something good to come out of the troubles. Following a major ceasefire brokered earlier this year between the government and fourteen rebel militias, groups of women came together across the nation to reinforce the grand strategy for peace at a community level. They were rebuilding their country from the ground up, forging formidable sisterhoods in the ashes of a protracted conflict.

High rates of sexual violence, maternal mortality and teenage births made CAR one of the worst places in the world to be a woman. But now female activists, displaced mothers and survivors of rape joined forces to heal deep wounds and restore trust between opposing ethnic factions as part of an ambitious attempt to mend a broken country in the heart of Africa.

Besides Abaka's bakers, another group called Femme Debout ("Woman Standing") defied religious tensions by bringing together Christian and Muslim widows in Bangui, CAR's capital, teaching them commercial skills and helping traumatized individuals recover collectively. Elsewhere, in camps for displaced people, where people shelter from militants who use sexual violence as a weapon of war, survivors enrolled with associations to fight the stigma of rape and to cultivate hope.

"Such groups are vital forces for social change," said Viola Giuliano, a researcher in CAR for the Center for Civilians in Conflict, an NGO focused on civilian protection. "They are uniquely placed to find and prioritize solutions and enable a sense of ownership of the peace process, which is key for sustainable, long-term reconciliation."

"At first the kids were scared of all these weapons, but now they're used to it," one of the bakers said. "But I do worry that the war will begin again. We've already lost so much. We cannot afford for it to happen again."

Despite these concerns she pressed ahead, along with seven friends, with what they do best. They rise at dawn and

congregate to scrub baking trays, gather large logs, chop up kindling and light fires in the kilns. Beneath a tin roof, they knead dough into hundreds of rolls. Small ones sell for the equivalent of 7p, a medium one for 14p, a loaf for 35p. Any profit is split between the women, allowing them to buy key household items and reinvest the remainder.

Revenues are modest; the impact, big. With almost half the country affected by acute food shortages and several regions teetering on the brink of famine, food production for malnourished communities is crucial. The bakers sell to local Muslim families, bringing once-divided communities together to intermingle in the marketplace. And in a place where the international response to a humanitarian crisis has received less than 50% of the funding it needs, a little extra cash represents a lifeline for struggling families.

Children are taught in a makeshift classroom at a camp in Kaga Bandoro that provides refuge for thousands of Central African families displaced by conflict

'These children are crucial': teaching forgiveness in CAR's besieged camps

"This bakery is the only opportunity we have to make any money by ourselves," says Estella Yarsara, Abaka's fellow baker and a 27-year-old mother of five. "This work means I have some extra food for my children too. I do this to help myself and to help my family. We all want to lift up our community."

The job has upended a conservative hierarchy, helping Yarsara challenge her role in society: "If I have some money and my husband does not, I can intervene and support him. It is making our relationship more equal. I don't have to depend on him. I have more strength in the family."

Another group of women run the Femme Debout women's association for widows and orphans in Bangui. Many of its members have suffered displacement and witnessed extreme violence, yet despite the war's divisions along religious lines, Christians and Muslims are welcomed alike.

Supported by UNHCR, the UN's refugee agency, the group meets every week on the edge of the capital to discuss their difficulties and successes. From sewing to soap-making, they are taught new skills, helping them foster solidarity and a boisterous, entrepreneurial spirit.

"Little by little women are getting together to fight back," said Atanguere, a mother of six who saw her brother stabbed to death when rebels stormed her neighborhood in late 2013. She fled to a squalid camp for displaced people and eventually returned home three years later, founding the association with the women she met there. "We are sisters. We are all Central Africans. It doesn't matter whether you're Muslim or Christian. Here, we are all equal."

While the worst of Atanguere's ordeal is over, more than 600,000 people remain displaced within CAR, with a similar number uprooted as refugees outside the country. Many of the women have been raped by militants. Yet among these exiled

communities, there is resilience and a restless desire to rise above such harrowing circumstances.

One of them is 18-year-old Céleste, who was five months pregnant when rebels attacked her village in northern CAR late one night. Gunshots and the roar of motorbikes woke her. "They raped many girls and tortured many men," said Celeste, just fifteen at the time of the attack. She wasn't spared either. Four soldiers entered her house, each taking turns to rape her: "My pregnancy was visible but they still did it anyway."

Afterwards, she fled her village and hid in the bush for several days, surviving on whatever she could find to eat. Her distress was amplified by memories of what she had lost. Before the war, she had enjoyed helping her father farm cassava, okra and peanuts, participating at school as an enthusiastic dancer and eager pupil. Now, forced from home, her sense of helplessness grew when she learned a few days later that her fiance – the father of her unborn child – had been murdered in the course of a car-jacking.

Céleste, whose name has been changed to protect her identity, eventually made it to a displacement camp on the outskirts of a rebel-held town called Kaga Bandoro. She moved into a cramped tent where she saw out the last few months of her pregnancy but could not shake off the psychological and physical pain of the attack. "Sleeping at night has been hard," she said softly. "It is difficult to forget. I miss my fiancé terribly." Yet even in this overcrowded and perilous camp, where armed groups freely operate, Céleste has started to overcome this nightmare. A friend introduced her to a

women's association where fellow survivors of rape enter a shared process of mutual healing and, together, tackle the stigma of sexual violence.

"I now feel that I have the strength to deal with what has happened," said Céleste. "The pastor at church teaches us to forgive, let go and move on. During therapy sessions, we can express ourselves. We talk about what has happened and discuss any problems that we still face."

Céleste and her fellow members are keen to return to school. Their dream: to take up midwifery and help pregnant mothers receive the care that war and poverty have denied them.

In spite of the camp's dangers and dreadful conditions, her son is now two years old and in relatively good health. With her country edging towards greater stability, Céleste clings to the hope of a life beyond their tiny, dusty tent – for now, the only home her child has ever known.

Situation elsewhere

During the height of the conflicts, women made up a large portion of the domestic workforce in Iran, replacing men who were fighting, injured, or dead. Women also played significant roles in lobbying for military veteran pension plans after the war.

Somali women in Mogadishu have formed NGOs which, among other activities, organize peace education for women. In the programme, women are first made aware of the cultural values and norms they convey to children in their everyday

interactions, and how these may contribute to discriminatory and violent behavior. Then they learn alternative forms of socialization that stress equity and social justice and non-violent ways of dealing with tensions and conflicts.

In **Rwanda**, dispossession among women survivors has become an acute problem. As the genocide decimated the male population, many women were left behind as single breadwinners without legal rights or access to land. In response to this highly precarious situation, some women have organized themselves and are demanding equal property rights. Others, who have access to land, "have now begun to form groups along the lines of pre-war associations, to help one another with agricultural production, to build houses, and to start up savings and credit schemes to finance income-generating activities".

Self-help organizations that aim primarily to help individuals and families in times of crisis can be found in many countries throughout the world. Recent studies of local-level post-war reconstruction in Angola, Chad, Eritrea, Ethiopia, Liberia and Sierra Leone suggest that they play an important role in post-war situations, in mobilizing resources and re-creating a sense of community, possibly also including marginalized social groups. However, it should be stressed that while self-help organizations are based on social cohesion and solidarity, war also reduces the integrity and capacities of such organizations Further, self-help organizations often lack the skills to become efficient intermediaries and managers of large-scale, long-term development projects. However, in Women and Post-Conflict Reconstruction Eritrea, for example, the *adi mahaber*

association has responded well in many areas to new requirements, and has proved to be an important mechanism for fund-raising for local development projects (Tommasoli, 1995). The association's success is due partly to its skill in reviving social relationships. Now, even if members of a community live in urban areas or abroad, they still contribute financially to development projects in their home villages. As a general word of caution, however, Tommasoli (1995: 26) warns that in Ethiopia "the grassroots community participation system is still ineffective due to the fact that women do not seem to be fully involved in decision-making processes within their households and communities".

In **Chad**, prior to the war, female kin occasionally organized an *azouma* party to raise money for major social events. After the war, female refugees returning to Chad revived this tradition, but turned it into a commercial business. The parties were now organized in public bars and restaurants, open to everyone. The result of this activity was Economic Reconstruction significant: "Income from the sale of drinks at the party enabled women to accumulate large sums of capital and strengthened ties of female solidarity beyond the immediate kin group" (Watson, 1996: 136). This initiative earned the women important sums for social events, but also provided them with capital for small development projects.

Recent studies on post-conflict Eritrea suggest that women's coping strategies are often linked to the expansion of economic activity in urban areas, which offer more and better opportunities. Bascom (1996), for example, states that in Eritrea, many women from rural areas have migrated to urban

areas to sell fruits and vegetables, handicrafts, beer, tea, and so on. They produce some of these items themselves, while others are obtained from wholesalers. Ahmed (1996) notes how a group of Eritrean women pooled their resources to open a fish market in the capital, Asmara. Another new economic opportunity is the raising of poultry, for which there is an increasing demand, especially in urban areas.

Post-war situations may also offer new areas of employment for women. One example is the international relief and development organizations that have become an attractive alternative source of income for the well-educated. The international attention to post-war reconstruction has also created new jobs indirectly, because many organizations favor a policy of channeling resources through local NGOs. Traditional self-help groups, community-based organizations, tribal organizations, and so on, transform themselves into NGOs, and previously unorganized groups of citizens now come together to obtain access to resources earmarked for local development projects (Taylor, 1995; Le Moal, 1997). The size of this new field relies partly on the history of state-civil society relations, and on the current space for action granted these organizations by the state. But even in countries with little experience of civil society organization, NGOs are now mushrooming in response to local needs and external priorities. One example is former Yugoslavia, where new NGOs emerge all the time, with women being particularly adept at adjusting to this new source of funding and employment (Le Moal, 1997). However, the large demand for skilled laborers in the emergency and immediate post-war period is likely to decrease with the return to mainstream

development work, in which case women may again face marginalization. The demand for NGOs as relief and development actors is also likely to decrease, as government institutions resume full capacity and new policies are effectuated, reducing the number of jobs in this sector.

In some countries, economic recovery may also introduce new areas of economic activity, which could mean more long-term employment opportunities for women. In Cambodia, for example, where women constitute 60 to 65 percent of the labor force, a new tourism industry is planned, which would increase women's employment opportunities considerably.

Tourism is also considered promising for women in Guatemala, and its partial recovery has already provided many women with an income from the production and sale of crafts (Marcus, 1996c). Many more countries with a war-shattered economy consider developing the tourism industry.

As the discussion of women's economic activities during and immediately after conflicts has clearly shown, women are economic actors, and important ones, too. As individuals and participants in self-help groups and extended networks, they not only make a contribution to the economic recovery of their families, but also play a major role in revitalizing the economic sphere at large.

Throughout history, women have made extraordinary contributions to their societies. Some have been recognized while most of them have been hushed in history dominated by men. Yet, there was nothing a man did without the support of a woman. Recognizing the achievements of women in all facets

of life has a huge impact on the development of self-respect and new opportunities for girls and young women. Discovering stories about our mothers, grandmothers, and great grandmothers help us to better understand their lives, the challenges they faced, and ultimately, ourselves and our times. Recognizing the dignity and accomplishments of women in our own families and those from other backgrounds leads to higher self-esteem among girls and greater respect among boys and men. The results can be remarkable, from greater achievement by girls in school to less violence against women, and more stable and cooperative communities. The impact of women's history might seem abstract to some, and less pressing than the immediate struggles of working women today. But to ignore the vital role that women's dreams and accomplishments play in our own lives would be a great mistake.

We draw strength and inspiration from those who came before us – and those remarkable women working among us today. They are part of our story, and a truly balanced and inclusive history recognizes how important women have always been in our society. This recognition will enable women to appreciate the roles of women in decision-making and political participation. Moreover, history can be a crucial tool in not only inspiring but also empowering women to come out in their numbers and participate in decision-making and politics. This is important because, despite the strong arguments in favor of increasing female participation in politics, women are still underrepresented in political decision-making around the

world. The international community has long recognized the importance of female representation, as shown by the Convention on the Elimination of all Forms of Discrimination against Women, the Beijing Declaration and Platform for Action, and UN Resolution 1325, among others. Most recently, this support has materialized in Sustainable Development Goal 5: achieve gender equality and empower all women and girls. Target 5 of SDG 5 reads: "Ensure women's full and effective participation and equal opportunities for leadership at all levels of decision-making in political, economic and public life." This target will be measured with indicators on the proportion of seats held by women in national parliaments and local governments, and the proportion of women in managerial positions. SDG 5.5 is directly linked to SDG 16.7, which embodies the commitment of all signatories to ensuring responsive, inclusive, participatory, and representative decision-making at all levels. Progress has thus far been slow on both targets.

It is also important to note that for too long, women were viewed as victims — of discrimination and illiteracy, of violence, and confined to deferential positions in society because of once-unbreakable cultural and religious traditions. But as the tide of democracy sweeps the globe, women are becoming a growing force on the world stage. We are seeing a new voice of activism emerge, which is speaking out to defend freedom and advance civil liberties and human rights. Some observers might assume that states, which previously treated women as second-class citizens, are becoming more just. Perhaps women are being treated more equally under the law,

gaining more respect in society, and acquiring greater power to shape political, economic, and social change.

Women have also proved to be vital players in peace and nation-building after armed conflicts as opposed to being remembered only as victims. It has been proven beyond any doubt that women participants in peace processes are usually focused less on the spoils of the war and more on reconciliation, economic development, education, and transitional justice – all critical elements of sustained peace. The inclusion of women can and must take many forms, especially in the effort to address rising global violent conflict that since the end of the Cold War has occurred within states, with armed insurgencies or civil wars tearing countries apart. The end to these conflicts cannot be forged through only a top-down peace process, with only armed actors at the negotiating table. Instead, it requires a more inclusive process—one that includes women playing more pivotal roles in building peace from the bottom up as well as from the top-down, engaging multiple stakeholders. Parties must come together not just in the capital city but also at the local level where communities are confronted with a host of critical issues that left unaddressed could unravel any peace deal.

Mary Nyakang and her colleague braided a client's hair – the salon, run entirely by widows, was the first one to open in Akobo town.
Source: Sam Mednick

Marsa Wanyag prepares dough at the bread-making shop in the town of Akobo.
Source: Sam Mednick

Pasca Kole, a refugee woman from South Sudan, with her daughter whom she
gave birth to shortly after arriving in Pagirinya Settlement in Uganda.
Source: UN Women/Aidah Nanyonjo

Members of a women's therapy group meeting in Pagirinya settlement share
stories and support one another.
Source: UN Women/Aidah Nanyonjo

Zeneba Simon chops kindling for the kilns at the bakery in Bamingui, Central African Republic, as Yvette Akaba (in white) and Estella Yarsara look on.
Source: Jack Losh

Chief baker Yvette Abaka stands outside her bakery in Bamingui.
Source: Jack Losh

BIBLIOGRAPHY

1. Separate spheres, Female worlds, Women's place: The rhetoric of women's history . Kerber, Linda K. 1988, The Journal of American History , p. 9.

2. 2. Is the feminist revolution still missing? Reflections from Women's history . Rupp, Leila J. 2006, Oxford University press , p. 10.

3. 3. Ansar Al-Sunna and Women's agency in Sudan: a Salafi approach to empowerment through gender segregation . Tonnessen, Liv. 2016, A journal of women studies , p. 21.

4. 4. A strategy for achieving Gender equality in South Sudan . Edward, Jane Kani. 2014, The Sudd Institute , p. 30.

5. 5. Power and Gender in ancient Egypt. la, Kristina Hilliard et. ancient history , s.l. : National art education Association , 2009, Vol. 62.

6. 6. Post-liberation state building in South Sudan. Bereketeab, Redie. 2014, Journal of African foreign affairs, p. 24.

7. 7. Women in the South African parliament: from Resistance to governance . Briton, Hannah Evelyn. 2005, University Illinois press, p. 41.

8. 8. Women's monumental mark on ancient Egypt. Lesko, Barbara S. History of women , Chicago : The University of Chicago Press , 1991, Vol. 54.

9. 9. Conclusion: civic morality in modern France . Allen, James Smith. Women in France, Nebraska : University of Nebraska , 2021.

10. 10. world society and the Nation-state . al, John W. Meyer et. sociology , Chicago : University of Chicago Press , 1997, Vol. 103.

11. 11. Statues, bodies and souls: St. Cecilia and some Medieval attitudes toward ancient Rome . Benson, C. David. Michigan : University of Michigan , 2017.

12. 12. Philo's language . Sly, Dorothy I. s.l. : Brown Judaic Studie , 2021.

13. 13. Mary Wollstonecraft and Adam Smith on gender, history, and the civic republican tradition. Leddy, Neven. Toronto : University of Toronto press, 2021.

14. Former Secretary of States Condoleezza Rice Talks Foreign Policy. https://ndsmcobserver.com/2019/10/condoleezza-rice-talks-global-policy/ Accessed 4.07PM on 22nd March 2022.

15. Why the United Nations Need More Female Peacekeepers. https://unu.edu/publications/articles/why-un-needs-

more-female-peacekeepers.html. Accessed on 22nd February 2022 at 9.54AM.

16. The Power of Women Peacebuilders.

    https://www.unwomen.org/en/news/stories/2019/10/compilation-the-power-of-women-peacebuilders. Accessed on 22nd February 2022 at 9.19 AM.

17. The Role of Women in Conflict Resolution Peace Building.

https://gsdrc.org/document-library/the-role-of-women-in-conflict-resolution-and-peacebuilding/#:~:text=There%20are%20obvious%20reasons%20why%20women%20are%20important%20to%20the%20peacebuilding%20process.&text=Women%20are%20also%20the%20central,peacekeepers%2C%20relief%20workers%20and%20mediators. Accessed on 22nd February 2022 at 9.20 AM.

18. Women in Peacekeeping: A key to peace-and a U.S. Priority-United States Department of States. https://2017-2021.state.gov/women-in-peacekeeping-a-key-to-peace-%CC%B6and-a-u-s-priority/index.html. Accessed on 22nd February 2022 at 9.17 AM.

19. Women in Peacekeeping |United Nations Peacekeeping.

https://peacekeeping.un.org/en/women-peacekeeping. Accessed on 22nd February 2022 at 9.15 AM.

20. The Essential Role of Women in Peacebuilding | United States Institute of Peace. https://www.usip.org/publications/2017/11/essential-role-women-peacebuilding. Accessed on 22nd February 2022 at 8.40AM.

21. The Role of Women in the Revolution

https://www.jstor.org/stable/41067045. Accessed on 22nd February 2022 at 8.26 AM.

22. Why Women's History? – National Women's History Alliance. https://nationalwomenshistoryalliance.org/why-womens-history/#:~:text=Recognizing%20the%20achievements%20of%20women,for%20girls%20and%20young%20women. Accessed on 22nd February 2022 at 8.04 AM.

23. Timelines: Women's Footprint in History. https://interactive.unwomen.org/multimedia/timeline/womensfootprintinhistory/en/index.html#intro1. Accessed on 22nd February 2022 at 8.01 AM.

24. Women in World History.

https://chnm.gmu.edu/wwh/. Accessed on 22nd February 2022 at 7.56 AM.

25. Women in Politics.

    https://www.goodreads.com/quotes/tag/women-in-politics. Accessed on 18th February 2022 at 5.53 PM.

26. The Role of Women in Promoting Peace and Development in the Horn of Africa.

    https://www.peacewomen.org/content/role-women-promoting-peace-and-development-horn-africa. Accessed on 18th February 2022 at 3.54PM.

27. Strengthening Women's Role in Building and Sustaining Peace.
    https://www.undp.org/speeches/strengthening-womens-role-building-and-sustaining-peace?utm_source=EN&utm_medium=GSR&utm_content=US_UNDP_PaidSearch_Brand_English&utm_campaign=CENTRAL&c_src=CENTRAL&c_src2=GSR&gclid=Cj0KCQiApL2QBhC8ARIsAGMm-KHBmZyn8G3bWqmy8mYh_WlmxYHwttlSu2Zhn wmyOFMcjo5oyzST0VIaAnAWEALw_wcB. Accessed on 18th February 2022 at 1.40 AM.

28. Wartime Sexual Violence. Accessed on 17th February 2022 at 1.09 PM.

29. Rape as a weapon of war: Women in South Sudan speak out.

https://www.euronews.com/2018/05/31/south-sudan. Accessed on 17th February 2022 at 11.44AM.

30. Still in Danger: Women and Girls Face Sexual Violence in South Sudan Despite Peace Deal.

   https://www.refugeesinternational.org/reports/2019/10/15/still-danger-women-girls-face-sexual-violence-south-sudan-peace-deal. Accessed on 17th February 2022 at 11.40AM.

31. Rape as a Weapon of War | Britannica.

   https://www.britannica.com/topic/rape-crime/Rape-as-a-weapon-of-war. Accessed on 17th February 2022 at 11.10AM.

32. Women and the Atrocities of War on JSTOR.

   https://www.jstor.org/stable/27879773. Accessed on 17th February 2022 at 9.54AM.

33. The Women's Revolution: Female Activism in Sudan. https://hir.harvard.edu/the-womens-revolution-female-activism-in-sudan/. Accessed on 16th February 2022 at 3.50PM.

34. Weaponization of Female Bodies: Rape as a weapon of war in the DRC.

   https://thesecuritydistillery.org/all-articles/weaponisation-of-female-bodies-rape-as-a-

weapon-of-war-in-the-drc. Accessed on 16th February 2022 at 2.55PM.

35. The Women's Rights Movements, 1848-1917 | US House of Representatives: History, Arts and Archives.

   https://history.house.gov/Exhibitions-and-Publications/WIC/Historical-Essays/No-Lady/Womens-Rights/. Accessed on 16th February 2022 at 2.07PM.

36. Brave: Meet the girls of South Sudan | Plan International UK

   https://plan-uk.org/blogs/brave-meet-the-girls-of-south-sudan. Accessed on 15th February 2022 at 5.45PM.

37. Wangari Maathai: Her activism saved forests, promoted peace. Video. https://www.csmonitor.com/World/Africa/2011/09 26/Wangari-Maathai-Her-activism-saved-forests-promoted-peace-video. Accessed on 15th February 2022 at 4.59PM.

38. Armed Afghan women take to streets in show of defiance against Taliban | Afghanistan | The Guardian.

   https://www.theguardian.com/world/2021/jul/07/a rmed-afghan-women-take-to-streets-in-show-of-

defiance-against-taliban. Accessed on 15th February 2022 at 4.56PM.

39. Women in Civil Rights Movement | Articles and Essays | Civil Rights History Project | Digital Collections | Library of Congress.

    https://www.loc.gov/collections/civil-rights-history-project/articles-and-essays/women-in-the-civil-rights-movement/. Accessed on 15th February 2022 at 4.51PM.

40. Civil War in South Sudan | Global Conflict Tracker.

    https://www.cfr.org/global-conflict-tracker/conflict/civil-war-south-sudan. Accessed on 15th February 2022 at 4.16PM.

41. Her War – Emma McCune in Sudan | The Mantle.

    https://www.themantle.com/literature/her-war-emma-mccune-sudan. Accessed on 15th February 2022 at 4.13PM.

42. African Female Warriors Who Led Empires and Armies – History.

    https://www.history.com/news/african-female-warriors. Accessed on 14th February 2022 at 3.24PM.

43. Unsung Heroines: Celebrating Women Who Inspire | Prosperity Candle.

https://www.prosperitycandle.com/blogs/news/uns ung-heroines-who-inspire. Accessed on 14th February 2022 at 2.44PM.

44. 10 Great Warrior Women of the Ancient World | History Hit.

   https://www.historyhit.com/10-great-female-warriors-of-the-ancient-world/. Accessed on 14th February 2022 at 2.01PM.

45. Ellen Johnson Sirleaf Ellen Johnson Sirleaf. Accessed on 10th February 2022 at 4.54PM.

46. The end of the African Women's Decade; tracking progress on commitments | Africa renewal.

   https://www.un.org/africarenewal/news/end-african-women%E2%80%99s-decade-tracking-progress-commitments. Accessed on 10th February 2022 at 12.23PM.

47. Feminist Foreign Policy –Feminist foreign policy. Accessed on 8th February 2022 at 5.48PM.

48. Women in Afghanistan worry peace accord with Taliban extremists could cost them hard-won rights.

https://theconversation.com/women-in-afghanistan-worry-peace-accord-with-taliban-extremists-could-cost-them-hard-won-rights-154149. Accessed on 8th February 2022 at 2.42PM.

49. Canada's Feminist International Assistance Policy.

https://www.international.gc.ca/world-monde/issues_development-enjeux_developpement/priorities-priorites/policy-politique.aspx?lang=eng#5.1. Accessed on 8th February 2022 at 2.40PM.

50. How a 'feminist foreign policy' could change the world

https://theconversation.com/how-a-feminist-foreign-policy-would-change-the-world-152868. Accessed on 8th February 2022 at 2.39PM.

51. Chapter 7: Women in Power and Decision-making – Global Women Issues: Women in the World Today; extended versions.

https://opentextbc.ca/womenintheworld/chapter/chapter-7-women-in-power-and-decisionmaking/. Accessed on 8th February 2022 at 2.05PM.

52. Most Influential Women in the World.

https://www.searchandshopping.org/web?q=most%20influential%20women%20in%20the%20world&o=1462011&rch=intl666&gclid=Cj0KCQiAxoiQBhCRARIsAPsvo-z-pU_POJOVwt38qhJxIzrWEeqMaDfLpc-8hn696oJHkpAlHmsa4b4aAqGPEALw_wcB&gclsrc

=aw.ds&qo=semQuery&ad=semA&ag=fw21&an=g oogle_s. Accessed on 8th February 2022 at 1.56PM.

53. Empowering Women at Work: Government's laws and policies for gender equality.

https://www.ilo.org/empent/Publications/WCMS_7 73233/lang--en/index.htm. Accessed on 8th February 2022 at 1.53PM.

54. Impact of Women's Participation in Decision-making. Accessed on 8th February 2022 at 1.29PM.

55. Six Women who Shaped the Contemporary World's Order | The Council on Foreign Relations.

https://www.cfr.org/blog/six-women-who-shaped-contemporary-world-order. Accessed on 7th February 2022 at 4.15PM.

56. 12 Women who Changed the World – ONE.

https://www.one.org/us/blog/12-women-who-changed-the-world/. Accessed on 7th February 2022 at 2.57PM.

57. These Bronze Age Women were more powerful than we thought – CNN.

https://edition.cnn.com/2021/03/10/europe/female-power-bronze-age-spain-scli-intl-scn/index.html. Accessed on 3rd February 2022 at 5.19PM.

58. Twelve Famous Women of the Middle Ages – World History Encyclopedia.

https://www.worldhistory.org/article/1350/twelve-famous-women-of-the-middle-ages/. Accessed on 3rd February at 5.19PM.

59. Women and Work: Fourteenth to Seventeenth Centuries – Renaissance and Reformation – Oxford Bibliographies.

https://www.oxfordbibliographies.com/view/document/obo-9780195399301/obo-9780195399301-0421.xml. Accessed on 3rd February 2022 at 4.03PM.

Made in the USA
Middletown, DE
18 July 2023

35421811R00135